THE COIN COLLECTIN

MW01153141

The Most Complete and Updated Guide from Beginners to Advanced to Buy and Sell the TOP Coins of All Time

Arthur K. Lindon

© Copyright 2022 - All rights reserved.

The content contained within this book may not be reproduced, duplicated, or transmitted without direct written permission from the author or the publisher.

Under no circumstances will any blame or legal responsibility be held against the publisher, or author, for any damages, reparation, or monetary loss due to the information contained within this book. Either directly or indirectly.

Legal Notice:

This book is copyright protected. This book is only for personal use. You cannot amend, distribute, sell, use, quote, or paraphrase any part, or the content within this book, without the consent of the author or publisher.

Disclaimer Notice:

By reading this document, the reader agrees that under no circumstances is the author responsible for any losses, direct or indirect, which are incurred as a result of the use of the information contained within this document, including, but not limited to, - errors, omissions, or inaccuracies.

The information contained in this book and its contents is not designed to replace or take the place of any form of medical or professional advice; and is not meant to replace the need for independent medical, financial, legal or other professional advice or services, as may be required. The content and information in this book have been provided for educational and entertainment purposes only.

Table of Contents

Introduction

For centuries, coin collecting has been a fun and rewarding hobby. It only takes a little research and knowledge to become an experienced collector who knows where to look for the best deals on coins and rare collectibles.

Coin collecting is more than just collecting coins; it is also about discovering and learning about history through coins and other collectibles without ever leaving your house.

The practice of numismatics, or the collection and analysis of coins, paper currency, medals, and tokens, offers the collector a variety of areas to focus on.

The prospect of becoming a coin collector is intriguing. The work itself appears simple; simply collecting old and new valuable coins. This may work if all you want is a stash of unclassified coins in a piggy bank or something, just like everyone else who throws their coins in a jar. It will not be visually appealing, and you cannot call this 'practice' coin collecting.

Understanding the ranking of different coins is critical before attempting to obtain the top-ranked coins from around the world. Only when you know which coin has the highest value will you be able to purchase it at a reasonable price.

Coins are collected for a variety of reasons. There are coin collectors who collect coins based on their expected future value. While some coin collectors do it for the metal diversity, others do it for the artifacts' historical significance.

If you're new to the hobby, it might be challenging to locate a trustworthy coin dealer from whom to purchase your coins. Someone doing this for a long time can be extremely helpful in directing you to a trustworthy and competent coin dealer. To begin, get a powerful magnifying lens and examine coins in a well-lit area for mintmarks, errors, and date readings on worn-out or damaged coins.

This guide contains instructions on how to get started with coin collecting so that you can avoid rookie mistakes that could jeopardize your practice and distort your collection. Learn about the different types of coins to collect, where to find them, and coin handling tips to keep them in good condition.

Coin collecting is an enthralling hobby because the marks on each coin reveal stories from the past. Each coin tells the story of the country in which it was issued, ranging from monarchy to great leaders to power and patriotism.

There are several ways and places to get started with your coin collection. To begin, search your old pockets for coins that you may have previously discarded. You may have traveled to other countries and discovered a wealth of unusual coins worth collecting. You can also visit coin shops in your neighborhood to find more valuable coins to add to your collection.

Read on and learn how to get a classic collection of your own that fascinates you and everyone who sees it. Who knows, it may be the greatest gift you leave for the next generation. Your valuable collection may even make you great money someday.

Book 1: Coin Collecting

What is Coin Collection?

Since the 12th century, coin collecting has been a popular hobby worldwide. There are various reasons for starting a coin collection, which collectors sometimes call 'numismatics.' Saving specific coins in your pocket change is one of the cheapest ways to begin collecting. After all, they will never go out of style and can be spent if you become dissatisfied with them.

Some collectors place value in holding a magnificent piece of handmade art in their palms, where they can elaborate on its age, history, and weight. Coin collecting is more than just a hobby for some people; it's a way of life. Rare objects are sought after and valued for their rarity and exquisiteness, often using metal sensors.

Whatever your reason for being interested in numismatics, understanding how things work is essential if you want to pursue it as a hobby. With so many different coins, starting a collection may be difficult. Before you invest money in coins, learn everything you can about them. Begin with the loose change in your pocket and learn about their pieces, images, engravings, material, and coin type. After you've learned the fundamentals, you'll be able to select the best method for building your collection.

Coin collecting is a fun hobby with a thriving community of collectors worldwide. Coins come in all shapes and sizes, and different collectors have diverse interests.

Coin collecting can be a rewarding and profitable hobby. There's something inherently appealing about a piece of cash that has been appraised at (often significantly) more than its original value and bears the history of its time.

Royalty, great leaders, history, power, and patriotism are frequently depicted on coins. For instance, Julius Caesar and Alexander the Great appeared on ancient coins, whereas Henry VIII, Napoleon, George Washington, and Abraham Lincoln appeared on contemporary coins.

Anyone, regardless of age or experience, can engage in coin collecting. Most collectors, however, begin when they are young. When children learn about the history of coins, they frequently notice how much money exists in the world. Many children are also curious about new things, such as lost treasure.

Others begin collecting coins when they find a unique coin in their change, inherit a collection, or acquire a few coins in other ways. Others think they've found a valuable and rare coin and are hoping to make a quick buck.

Coin collecting can be a perplexing hobby when you start at first, especially when there appears to be so much to learn about it.

History of Coin Collection

After the terrible Wall Street crash of 1929, it was believed that the only assets of interest to anxious investors during the Great Depression were rare cars, exquisite art, and traditional coins. That rule of thumb has appeared to be true since the 1930s during each successive period of economic turmoil, where the three groups above have repeatedly affirmed their value.

Some gold and silver coins are rare in the world of collectibles because they have characteristic worth based on their valuable metal content and historical position. Global monetary markets recognize the melt worth of silver and gold, but valuable metal bars are not accepted for their beauty or rarity only.

For as long as coins have been formed, people have stored them for their bullion value. On the other hand, coin collecting for its creative worth was a future phenomenon. Researchers and state treasuries collected and classified coins according to an archeological and historical indication from Early Rome and feudal Mesopotamia.

Individuals may have also collected traditional, odd, or commemorative coins as an inexpensive and transportable art form.

Coin collecting and appreciation, as we know them today, were initiated during the 14th century, during the Renaissance period. Coin gathering became the "interest of kings" because it could only be afforded by the exceptionally rich. Petrarch, an Italian researcher and poet, is recognized as the pioneer and most well-known sports lover. Many European royals, princes, and nobility followed his principal and collected antique coin assortments.

Coin collecting continued as a patrician activity in the 17th and 18th periods. Nevertheless, during Europe's so-called Era of Enlightenment in the 18th century, a more systematic approach to collecting and perusing historical coins was established. On the other hand, Coin collection became a predominant activity among the growing middle class, who wanted to authenticate their prosperity and intellect.

The coin marketplace grew in the 19th and 20th-century periods to include antique coins and foreign and exotic currencies. During these decades, coin exhibitions, trade links, and controlling bodies arose, and in 1962, the American Numismatic Association hosted the first international coin gatherers' conference in Michigan. A projected 40,000 people joined, representing the appeal of the coin collection that was once linked to the richest and most noble.

While it is tough to guess the number of coin collectors, it is deceptive that coins today attract people of all ages and backgrounds. Between 1999 and 2008, the US Mint prophesied that 120 million Americans chased the 50 States Quarters. This number proves that, despite its origins, coin collection has changed into one of the most democratic hobbies, with entry-level prices so that even children can have enough money to join in on the fun.

Who Collects Coins?

Who exactly is able to be a coin collector may be an even more important myth to dispel. Coin collecting is typically linked with the extremely wealthy, perhaps because of the stereotype of the Victorian gentleman interested in antiques.

That isn't always the case, though.

Coin collecting is actually one of those hobbies today that appeals to a wide range of social classes, age ranges, and general interests. Today, anyone can become a coin collector, whether they are young or old, an artist or an engineer.

Who collects coins? It could be any of the following:

A traditional hunter typically has a list before they leave and never deviates from it. This collector is methodical and reliable, and they typically won't give up until they've finished everything on their list. A speculator only gathers in order to increase his initial investment. As a general rule, I wouldn't advise doing this because coin collecting may be about much more than making money, especially for beginners.

The aesthetic collector will mostly gather coins because of their aesthetic appeal. For this kind of collector, the condition of the coins can be more important than their assessed value.

The perfectionist will always look for coins that are perfect in every way. They want the coin to appear flawless, valuable, and in excellent condition.

The budget collector will strive to amass as much as they can and is constantly on the lookout for savings. His primary criterion is price, and he will hoard coins simply because they are inexpensive.

The collector who does this to boast is the presenter. In his home, he will build an entire altar just for his coins, and he will take every opportunity to display them for anybody he invites.

Sometimes the academic collector is also a numismatist (at least at an amateur level). Along with coins, he'll amass a plethora of knowledge about them, enough to write an entire book about them.

Coins are historical artifacts, so the historian collector will collect coins. Coins are the living evidence of a bygone era, and this type of collector will develop an almost emotional attachment to his coins.

The patriot will primarily collect coins related to his country's history. Most of the time, the same person will collect other items related to his country.

You could, of course, develop into a different kind of collector who does not necessarily fit into any of the categories mentioned above. The main goal of explaining them was not to assist you in "picking" a typology but rather to help you comprehend the variety of coin collectors and the fact that this is a hobby that can truly be enjoyed by anyone.

Reasons for Coin Collection

Making Money

Coin collection can also be utilized to expand your investment portfolio. A trustworthy coin trader can support you and add worth to your portfolio by vending rare silver and gold. Many experts will tell you that investing in valuable bullion coins can help you decrease your risk. In addition, if you need money, you may sell your coin collection effortlessly.

The Challenge

It is our nature to want to explore things comprehensively. When we see a job or a goal done, it gives us a feeling of achievement. Successful coin collectors begin by determining what they wish to gather. When we find the perfect coin for our collections, the "excitement of the pursuit" sometimes brings us happiness. Finding a valued coin in your pocket change can also offer satisfaction. Lastly, one of the utmost pleasant features of such an activity is the gratification of possessing a valued coin collection.

Art and Beauty

Each coin's design starts with the gifted hands of an artist. Although many types of artists can make coins, those who comprehend the importance of the whole procedure are the best on most occasions.

Most numismatists think the Saint-Gaudens double eagle Saint-Gaudens was the most attractive USA currency ever made and came out around 1907-1933. In the same way, David Brenner's Lincoln cent by David Brenner and The UNA by William Wyon is among the other marvels with a huge reputation among the masses.

In this way, one can say that coin collections are indeed art collections. The proprietor of an accurately curated coin gathering will desire to display their valued belongings proudly.

Education and History

Nearly every coin has a historical factor. It may portray the victory of an old war memorialized on an ancient US coin, the coronation of a king on a primitive coin, or a socializing memorial coin depicting each of the 50 USA States.

Colonial coins that entered the USA before the official formation of the United States Mint in 1792 are significant remnants of history. The same can be said about pirate coins recovered from momentous wreckages. World coins can support you learn about diverse countries and values worldwide.

Make a Lasting Impression

A well-planned and well-invested coin gathering can be a great legacy for your successors. Even though few people get rich by collecting coins overnight, well-organized and ingenious investing plans in rare and valuable coins can grow in worth over time.

Try to increase the attention of your children in coin collecting. Most kids lose interest in coin collecting around adolescence, although some might pick it back up years later. They will be able to look back on your Heritage in your coin gathering in years to come. They may even recall getting an exclusive coin from you.

Relaxation

Putting together a coin collection and investigating the history of a specific piece can support you in overlooking the strain and pressures you face throughout the day. Coins are simple to gather and can be found in your pocket, at a preferred coin shop, at a coin demonstration, or on the Internet.

Popularity

According to many personalities, coin collecting is becoming more prevalent in the Western world. People have observed their republic's mint production of "exclusive" coins for specific events. People buy them, believing they are valued. While they have worth beyond their apparent value, it is often unimportant.

Other Investment Alternatives

Equities, Real estate, and bonds are just a few instances of many sorts of investments. While these are all rock-hard investments by most, they may not be the finest fit for you.

Maybe these options don't increase your consideration, or you don't think they are a valuable investment. Coin collecting, instead, could be a greater investment for you.

Legacy

You most likely do not trust that your coin collection will ever be worth anything. Nevertheless, if you continue enhancing your collection each year, it will eventually upsurge exponentially.

You will acquire a small fortune in ancient coins, in terms of their appearance and numismatic value, if you do this throughout your working life and perhaps even into retirement.

These collections may become your Heritage. Virgil Brand, Harry Bass, and Louis Berg are all gone. They do, nevertheless, recall the enormous coin collections they left behind.

Where To Locate Coins

Coin collecting is a fun pastime. First and foremost, have a glance in your pocket; it is the ideal location for coin collecting. Before spending money with your pocket change, separate the attractive coins. Coins can also be obtained via various sources, including coin stores, coin shows, the internet and mail orders, and fellow collectors.

Coin Shops

These coin shops are excellent resources for learning about coins and coin collecting. These coin shops may be pricey since they want to sell their coins for a profit. You can receive great rates for your coins if you have enough knowledge and someone who knows a lot about coin collecting on your side.

Coin Shows

Occasionally, a display of numerous coin sellers will be set up in your local mall. These will allow you to view their collection and purchase a few at a discounted price due to competition. Several new coins will almost certainly be available for purchase and would make excellent additions to your collection. These coin exhibits are fantastic for collectors and coin enthusiasts looking to see rare and difficult-to-find coins.

Web Sites/Mail Orders

There are many dealers all over the world, and the most of them have websites where you may order through the mail or pay online using a service like PayPal. You should research these companies and carefully read their rules to ensure you can get your money back if you have issues with the coin you received. There is certainly a slew of fraudulent websites vying for your money for every genuine website. Before you pay anyone online, get feedback and make sure you don't give out passwords or PINs.

Markets of All Kinds

These are the markets where you can buy and sell. This type of website is an unexpected source of rare coins. Nonetheless, these areas have different price perceptions because of their lack of understanding of how a coin is valued. You will come across expensive coins; however, if you are lucky, you may come across a one-of-a-kind coin among the piles of coins, making it worthwhile. Sellers at flea markets usually want to make a quick buck, so buying in bulk will almost always result in a discount. Try to buy other things to get your coin as a bonus.

Auctions

If you want to buy scarce coins, you should go to an auction. Only at auctions will you find people selling their most valuable and unusual coins. Many of these auctions take place online, and most sellers seek the highest bidders. However, you should be warned that some of these sellers are con artists who won't justify the cost you pay. Before you try to purchase one from an online auction, you should learn more about these coins and their values.

Coin Dealers

Coin dealers are the most secure way to begin collecting coins. Even in this case, you must ensure you purchase your coins from a reputable coin dealer. Your best bet is to deal with Professional Numismatists Guild (PNG)-approved dealers. This means they will follow very strict rules regarding the coins they sell and how much they sell.

National Coin Exhibitions

National coin shows, like local coin shows, can be a treasure trove of finds for avid collectors. The same rules apply here: avoid anything that could raise suspicions and only buy from reputable, accredited dealers.

International Treaties

Suppose you are more interested in collecting coins from around the world. In that case, you will almost certainly need to attend a few international conventions to connect with dealers who have coins from countries other than the United States.

Additional Collectors

Connecting with like-minded people is another excellent way to collect coins. This will allow you to discuss your hobby, learn more about it, exchange coins, and even buy them from collectors who have either changed their hobby or are looking to make a profit.

Joining the American Numismatic Association is one way to meet people who share your interests. This membership is not free, but it is reasonably priced (especially compared to the benefits it would offer you).

Also, you can find other coin collectors by joining a local or regional coin club. This will allow you to meet with peers regularly, discuss, and exchange knowledge and coins.

Collecting Method and Approaches

To be honest, there is no correct or incorrect technique to collect coins. Because this is a hobby for most people, the regulations should never be taken seriously. Sure, there are some things to be aware of that you must keep in mind. Beyond that, you have complete control over how you acquire and organize your coins. Stay informed and keep your eyes peeled.

You can put together a collection of coins that are becoming increasingly valuable in terms of their intrinsic value and what you previously had in your collection. Many novice coin collectors begin by evaluating a larger collection and then reducing it to what they are most interested in.

Give yourself time and patience because it's challenging to know precisely what you want immediately, especially if this is all new to you. Nobody is forcing you to do anything; patience is the key lesson we can take from these coins, which have been there for hundreds, if not thousands of years.

If you're looking for some ideas on how to collect and organize your collection, consider the following suggestions:

- *Sort them into denominations*. This implies that you will combine all of a currency's distinct denominations. You'll probably start with a shorter time range, but if you find that this strategy appeals to you more than others, you can easily expand to decades or entire eras.

- **Sort them into categories.** You can even limit yourself to collecting a specific coin within a given denomination. You can also expand to other denominations if you want to.

- **Sort them by the date they were collected.** This means you'll be collecting coins of the same denomination for several years. For example, you could begin by collecting all of the denominations from the year you were born until now.

  Then you can elaborate as you see fit. Sort them according to the date and mintmark combination. This can be more expensive because it instantly makes the coins you seek rarer.

- **Sort them into years.** For instance, you might want to amass every coin you were given at birth. You can make this a decade-long project or collect pennies from around the world from the year you were born.

- **Sort them into categories.** This is a wonderful way to start coin collecting, and it may even be interesting for kids. For instance, you might decide to start collecting all president-themed coins from the United States before moving on to the rest of the world.

- **Sort them according to the mintmark.** This may be a little more challenging for a beginner due to the rarity of particular mintmarks, but it is not impossible.

- **Gather them by chance.** Many collectors, believe it or not, are anxious to get all the errors from a certain period or currency. Why don't you do it as well?

- **Sort them according to their rarity.** Generally speaking, this will cost more because all the coins you wish to add to your collection are probably expensive and scarce.

- **Sort them into countries.** Country-based coin collections, like themed collections, can be fun for youngsters since they can learn about different parts of the world.

- **Sort them by time period.** You might focus your coin collection on a specific historical period if you are fascinated by or attached to it. For example, you could amass all World War I coins from the United States and/or the rest of the world.

- **Sort them into groups based on their design.** Some people sort and collect coins based on the main design theme. For example, you can come across collections dedicated solely to animals, flowers, or sports.

- **Sort them according to the metal they're made of.** For instance, buying gold or silver coins could be more expensive, but the good news is that you can keep adding to your collection as you set new objectives. For example, you may start with all silver coins released in the United

States up to a given period and broaden your attention to the entire world. You can also extend the period of your interest and then move to non-US currencies.

Coin collection is a long-term game, so have fun while you're at it. Additionally, even while the majority of collecting techniques might yield respectable earnings, there's no need to concentrate on one technique solely because it's more lucrative or because someone else insists you must collect coins a certain way.

Tools for Coin Collection

As your interest in coin collecting grows, you'll want to invest in some coin collecting gear and tools to help you put your collection together. While not exhaustive, the following items will help you become a more efficient and thorough coin collector:

- Nitrile gloves or any pair of gloves
- Jewelry loupe
- A gram scale
- A magnet
- A digital microscope
- Reference books related to coin collection

These instruments are required for coin collection.

Nitrile Gloves or Any Pair of Gloves

Because sometimes coins are so filthy, they are handled using nitrile gloves. They're useful when you're looking at many coins at once. You'll be surprised at how filthy your hands become after touching coins. Powder-free gloves are advisable. They come in a variety of sizes, so choose wisely. You'll be glad you did if you order 100. They are available in black and blue.

Gram Scale

When it comes to weighing money, a gram scale is a must-have. The capacity of these little scales is 8 ounces. To determine authenticity, metal content, and mistake types, certain coins must be weighed. Make sure the scale you buy is accurate to the hundredth of a gram.

Magnet

A powerful magnet is utilized to identify counterfeit coins. Even if something doesn't stick to the magnet, it could still be false gold, fake silver, or a counterfeit coin. If someone tries to sell you a gold or silver coin that adheres to the magnet, you know it's not genuine.

Coin Magnifiers & Loupes Magnifier Loupe

Every numismatist should own a star magnifier. These are necessary to determine a coin's worth, find flaws and problems, check for error coins, and discover counterfeits. It's practical and sensible to have a solid magnifier at home and a pocket magnifying or jeweler's loupe on the go. The majority of collectors prefer magnification of 10x to 20x.

Reference Books for Coin Collection

You'll also need a reference book to identify your coins and determine their value. If you're interested in collecting coins, you'll want to have at least one book covering the basics, like mintmarks, dates, and notable varieties. Further reading on various related topics, such as how to detect counterfeits or different die varieties, can be highly beneficial. Prices and news will be more up-to-date in periodicals. By helping you avoid making poor decisions, good reference books can pay for themselves many times over. Experts regard this list of references as a good starting point.

One of the following options might be a good fit for you:

- ***Red Book - A Guidebook of United States Coins:*** This is the standard price guide for U.S. coins from the colonial era, as presented in the brochure. Collectors can expect to pay up to these prices for specific coins from a vendor. To learn everything there is to know about coin collecting, pick up a copy of this book. There should be a copy in every collection, and it is released annually.
- ***Standard Catalog of World Coins:*** This catalog lists the values of coins from the 20th century. This is an excellent resource for learning about different world coins.
- ***Coin Collectors Survival Manual:*** Coin collectors will find a wealth of new information in this book written by a coin expert. Coin collecting topics have been discussed amusingly.

Book 2: How to Make Money

Choose first whether you want to sell the coin through an auction house or do it yourself and sell it on eBay, at a coin exhibition, or anywhere else.

When you have higher grades and quality or uncommon items, an auction may be the best option, but remember that you will pay a significant seller's fee in most cases.

Recently, many people have begun trading their coins on eBay. That could be a better platform depending on the circumstances, but before you choose that over selling to a dealer, I would advise you to do some calculations. Selling on eBay may include selling fees, listing fees (typically 9%), insertion fees in some cases, and the cost of shipping and insuring your item, which can be substantial for valuable coins. The time it takes to write a good listing and the reasons you should wait to see if the item sells are also factors. If it doesn't, you still owe the insertion and listing fees.

This leaves many people with the option of selling to a dealer - either your local dealer, at a coin show, or through the mail, if you deal with the main dealer who buys similar to the APMEX. You will most likely get it at a reasonable price if you carefully select a reputable dealer with extensive experience.

The buy-sell margins vary greatly, depending on the type of coin you intend to sell. If you have something that will take a long time for the dealer to sell and a lot of them, you will get something smaller. You might want to try someone who specializes in that type of coin, as they might be willing to pay more.

You could be able to get a price that is at least equal to what you would get if you sold a popular precious metal coin with a challenging wholesale market, such PCGS and NGC graded generic pre-1933 gold or superior modern U.S. Mint products with low mintages.

Dealers generally buy and sell such coins on very low margins and make their money through the volume; however, a higher profit on lower-end items is required to compensate for the additional time required to sell them. Remember that rather than attempting to advertise the coin in their store or on their website, you are frequently marketing to a dealer who can likely wholesale the coin to another dealer for a little profit.

Generally, your dealer pays a bid or a small underbid for good coins that sell quickly and a lower amount for coins that take longer to sell as the lower-end coin collector. A different method of determining the amount a dealer pays for a coin you want to sell is to visit the websites of some major retailers, who occasionally post their buying prices for items they need.

Finally, remember that many people are unaware that the coin market is rotational and that profiting takes time.

One must be patient, examine the market correctly, and recall that when you aim to maximize your return, you may be required to hesitate for the market so your particular item can be improved.

The Perfect Time to Sell Coins

When is the ideal chance to sell coins? This might be an idiotic inquiry whenever posed of a mint piece collector, but the timing makes a distinction. Sometimes a coin collector wakes up in the morning and decides on the spur of the moment to sell his priceless collection of coins. When a collector must occasionally give up their mint piece collections for private reasons, selling their priceless coins is often the most difficult part. Regardless of the reasons, this occurs in the life of a mint piece collector.

There are numerous reasons why mint piece collectors sell their currencies – some are vendors. Selling coins is their choice, and they may utilize it to create a pay to procure different coins they like.

A few collectors travel to find the mint piece they need, and while they are moving around, they may come across currencies that are not suitable for their collection, but they nevertheless manage to acquire them. When they return, they sell the coins they have acquired and use the proceeds to buy the coins they are looking for.

Additionally, mint piece collectors accumulate currencies, unlike their pastimes; these mint piece collectors utilize the coins as their wellspring of salary. They get by selling the mint pieces that they gather. They occasionally give the mint pieces to various collectors and place a larger value on them than the going rate for the currency. This is fitting if the collector claims restricted versions or uncommon coins.

Then again, a few collectors sell their coins due to different components. They may sell coins given individual reasons. Since they are forced to sell their collection of coins, some collectors occasionally decide to "part with" their collection. This is the most troublesome circumstance for mint piece collectors as they frequently esteem their currencies and, however much as possible, would not have any desire to part with them – the currencies might be memorabilia or have a nostalgic incentive to them.

When a coin collector decides to sell his collection, he should think about whether this is the best time to do so. Is the collector prepared to part with his coins? Is the coin at a more significant expense now? Will it progress nicely, and will he profit by selling his coins? These components should consistently be thought of.

To choose where a mint piece collector could sell his coins, there are various options available. He could have to barter the coins for cash. Numerous individuals presently lean toward making their assets available to be purchased, which isn't constrained to mint piece assortments.

Since barters include offering forms, there is also a greater chance that the coin will be sold for a higher price. Purchasers may offer at a greater expense, mainly if the coin sold is of uncommon quality and has a higher worth.

In order to advertise the coins he might want to sell, a collector may also need to create a website. The Internet is the least demanding route for collectors to look for coins. What's more, putting the coin on the Internet will make selling a simpler undertaking. The authority may set up his site and spot the photos of his coins and some concise portrayals. He should likewise note the amount he is willing to sell them for.

There are also different choices: the merchant might need a vendor-to-seller exchange. He can legitimately go to coin vendors and sell his coins. At that time, the vendors can sell the coins they purchased to other vendors.

It is imperative to consider costs between one seller and another as there is consistently an opportunity for one vendor to purchase the coins at a more significant expense than other sellers. It is shrewd to look for vendors and choose which one you need to manage.

Additionally, collectors who choose to sell their coins utilize a coin reviewing administration. It is signed with the goal that the dealer does not end up in a washout when he sells his coins. By utilizing an evaluating administration, the dealer will have the option to set a value that depends on the appraisal made by the reviewing administration, who will decide the genuine estimation of the coins.

Once currency authorities have decided to sell their coins, they shouldn't refine them.

Money Making Strategies Used by Coin Collectors

Although there are many such strategies, five of them stand out as more common (and generally successful).

Buy and Hold

This is one of the most traditional approaches to making a profit from your coin collection. Like in the stock example, this strategy involves buying coins, holding them until their value appreciates, and then selling them. This strategy is mostly more suitable for long-term players (such as people who might invest in coins for their retirement portfolio, for example).

Buy Blue Chips

Blue Chips are coins with a large target audience and continuously appreciate value. These are usually very popular with coin collectors ranging from beginners to experts. Because they are relatively rare, however, they keep on appreciating year after year.

Buying blue chips is another good long-term strategy for those who are not looking to make profits very soon. You might be able to make some profit in one or two years, but in these situations, the longer you wait, the more profit you can make.

Watch the Inflection Points

This strategy is similar to stock market momentum investment and is usually recommended for collectors and investors with some field experience.

In (very) short, this strategy involves buying on the downgrade side of rising inflection points. These inflection points are moments (or grades) when the demand increases and pushes the retail price (sometimes even doubling it). If you can predict when this happens, you can wait for the perfect moment to sell coins at a very high-profit margin.

Remember that this might not always happen to high-grade coins (such as uncirculated ones). This is because the market already believes these coins are fairly valued.

Use a Large Collector Base

This strategy involves looking for, buying, and selling affordable coins to the average collector. Because this will considerably broaden your target audience, there is a higher likelihood that you will be able to sell your coins faster and make profits. The profit you make for each coin you sell might not be shockingly high, but if you scale this to multiple coins, you can make a well-rounded sum of money.

Cherry Pick

This strategy is the exact opposite of the previously mentioned one. Cherry-picking coins means choosing a very narrow target audience to address and trying to make the most out of the coin cycle movement (which we will discuss in the next section of this chapter). By buying when the prices are at their lowest and finding your target audience at the exact moment when the prices reach their high, you can easily make some serious profits out of your coin-selling activity.

Buy or Find

You can choose these two options when deciding how to obtain coins for your collection. Each option has charm, difficulty, and satisfaction as you try to find a particular coin you have been dreaming about.

Finding a coin involves hard work, but it can also be fun and may give you more satisfaction when you finally obtain it. This may be likened to an archeological expedition. You may get the same satisfaction if you buy, but it could involve more monetary expense. Neither option takes away from the other, whatever way you choose. If you are collecting coins based on a series or type and are having trouble finding them, you may be forced to buy them to complete your collection.

Pricing

Coin prices, like any commodity, are subject to the law of supply and demand. The availability of coins is referred to as supply - how many are available right now? How many of these coins were produced? The number of coin collectors looking for this or that coin is called demand. Many rare US coins are in high demand because many collectors want to add them to their collections.

Prices rise when coins cannot be moved at current levels and will continue to rise if current demands are not met. However, there are times when prices are unaffected by market forces. For example, a buyer or seller is unaware of current prices and trends.

Coin collectors and investors are the ones who determine current coin demand. Dealers must also account for demand because they must sell the coins in their inventory to make a profit. Dealers sell their coins at retail prices to collectors and investors while selling at wholesale prices to one another.

Dealers typically pay less than wholesale when purchasing coins from the general public or other collectors and investors to make a profit. As a result, you should be aware that you may not receive the expected profit if you decide to sell your coins to a dealer.

If you are a buyer, you should go to someone knowledgeable and can guarantee the authenticity of the coin you are purchasing, which is a dealer. You would avoid a seller who knows nothing about what they are selling.

Any coin is worth the amount of money you are willing to pay. But what is a reasonable price? Many factors must be considered when determining what a buyer will accept as a fair price. Aside from the previously mentioned supply and demand factors, the following must be considered:

- **Identification** - country of origin, face value, date, and, if applicable, mintmark, design
- **Authenticity** - this must be determined by an expert and is required for rare coins.
- **Grade** - a coin's overall condition, whether the mint state (new) or circulated (used.)
- **Coin cleaning and other damage** – the coin must not have been cleaned or polished, corroded, scratched, or altered.
- **Bullion value** - the value of the precious metals used to make the coin.

Price Lists

Once you've determined how much a coin is worth, you may need to consult price guides to determine the typical going prices for a specific coin type or series. Several coin price publications are available.

- **Chester L. Krause and Clifford Mishler's Standard Catalog of World Coins** - This contains information on and prices for coins from around the world in four volumes, each covering a separate century from 1601 to 2000.
- **A Guide Book of US Coins** - published annually; commonly used to determine retail price guides and other useful information.
- **Coin World, Coin Prices, and Coin Age** - regularly published retail prices for US coins.
- **The Coin Dealer Newsletter** - also known as "the Graysheet," is the ultimate price guide for dealer-to-dealer transactions.
- **A Handbook of United States Coins** - colloquially known as "the Blue Book,"; this is another resource for dealers who buy US coins from the general public.
- **Numismatic News** - This lists the buy, bid, and retail prices for all three dealers.

You can find these publications and others that deal with coin prices in libraries, bookstores, and coin shops. There are also many online sources of information that you can find on the World Wide Web.

Tips for Buying Coins

Fruitful coin collectors devote a significant amount of effort to learning everything there is to know about numismatics. Newsletters, magazines, and brokers who can provide information and news as it happens are good sources of information. By utilizing the available resources, a person may move quickly before new collectors with the same desire receive information.

If an individual attempts to gather without first learning the fundamentals, he will fail miserably. A collector's ability to evaluate coins might help them determine the true worth of their collection.

This information will be useful if the owner selects to exchange for something of higher value or help prevent scams and squandering money on something of low value. Always be on the lookout! Because a coin collection might take years to complete, one of the virtues that coin collecting can teach is patience.

Several world's most well-known collectors have waited years to reap the benefits. It's crucial to develop coin collector mentality. Too much excitement is bad because a collector may be enticed to acquire or exchange the incorrect coin, which could be pricey. Even if the information originated from a trusted source, think twice before using it.

Collecting coins can be difficult, mainly for those just getting started. A person's budget is unlikely to allow him to purchase articles worth more than $10,000, so it's best to start a small market investigation for 3 to 6 months before pursuing the largest prizes.

Coin collecting is parallel to sports. It takes time to master, and immediate and longstanding goals must be demonstrated. Any person could join the ranks of other expert coin collectors by following the guidelines and employing common sense.

The Best Places to Buy Coins

The best site to buy coins is determined by the type of coins you collect and how you collect them. Some people began collecting coins after discovering something unusual in their pocket change. Others begin collecting coins after inheriting a coin collection. Some people are initiated to coin collecting by a friend or relative. Regardless of how you begin your coin-collecting quest, you will eventually need to buy coins to complete your collection. Almost every coin collector fantasizes about turning a little fortune when they sell their collection. This objective will be easier to fulfill with education and proper planning.

On the other hand, people hoping to earn a quick buck are frequently disappointed. You'll have greater luck as a New York Stock Exchange day trader than flipping coins for a quick buck. No matter how much money you make when you sell your collection, collecting coins is a hobby that you will enjoy for the rest of your life.

You may buy coins from anybody and anywhere but be cautious. In your pursuit of a good deal, you may end yourself overpaying for coins or getting ripped off. Take your time and avoid typical coin-collecting blunders. Every coin collector, no matter how much time and effort they put into researching their acquisitions, has made one or more mistakes while purchasing coins. The intelligent coin collector will learn from their errors and utilize that information to construct a more valuable collection in the long term.

The internet may appear to be a coin collector's paradise, with discounts on every screen. However, the internet is like the Wild West, with numerous scammers and robbers waiting to take advantage of you. When buying any coin via the Internet, extreme caution should be observed.

The Cycles of the Coin Market

The coin market is easy to understand, as it is mainly connected to supply and demand. The supply is limited and decided by the government emitting the coins, while the demand is flexible and can be influenced by some factors.

Assume there are only 50 pieces of a particular coin. If there are 100 buyers, the price will rise. The price will fall if there are 40 buyers. Suppose someone (for example, an entity) decides to promote the coin and tout its incredible value. In that case, the number of interested buyers will likely multiply several times over (depending on how great the promotion was). When this happens, the market becomes unbalanced, and the price of that coin can skyrocket.

Let's look at a specific example. The 1974 Silver Dollar sold for no less than $10 million, a large sum (probably shocking enough) to break through the closed collectors' circle and into mainstream media (Reaney, 2013).

As a result, demand for all Mint State Bust Dollars increased overnight, making them more valuable (even if they were graded lower). On the other hand, a wise investor would recognize that this is a temporary state and either take advantage and buy before the wave of interest rises or ignore the opportunity and look for one that follows a similar pattern.

It may sound like gambling, but the coin market is far more predictable than Russian roulette or a game of poker. It is not always possible to "smell" the right opportunity, but it is well worth the effort.

Understanding how the coin market works behind the scenes can help you bargain with coin dealers, whether buying or selling coins. One of the most important concerns I've observed as a coin collector is the stark difference between what the typical client expects from a coin dealer and what the typical coin dealer believes he should provide to the consumer. Most of these distinctions are founded on trust.

The average customer believes he can trust the coin dealer to provide an accurate appraisal and a fair price for his selling coins. The average dealer believes it is his responsibility to pay the lowest possible price for the coins to maximize his profit. The consumer must conduct research on his own. Fortunately, by gathering this information, you will be better prepared to deal with coin sellers.

Overview of the Coin Dealing Industry

The two main types of coin traders are wholesalers and retailers. The distributor actively seeks new material to enter the market, frequently attending coin shows and local auctions, and running advertisements to buy coins. The bulk of this product is sold to retail-based dealers. Put another way, they buy coins from anyone but only sell them to other dealers. Unfortunately, these merchants must pay lower prices to profit from their sales.

Wholesalers supply the majority of the stock for the retail coin dealer. Retail coin dealers may attend coin fairs and shop locally, but the majority of their income comes from serving individuals who only want to buy one coin. Since your coins won't have to go through two sets of hands before being sold, a dealer of this kind is more likely to offer you a higher price for them. However, remember that certain local sellers are frequently the worst offenders! This is so because bigger dealers are more likely to belong to groups like the Professional Numismatists Guild or the American Numismatic Association, which obligate them to abide by a Code of Ethics. The most important consideration for anyone buying or selling coins is recourse. What are your options if something goes wrong?

This is not to say that all coin dealers are bad people—quite the opposite. Most coin dealers follow principles and morals to protect their future businesses. A few bad apples, on the other hand, can shake your faith in the coin-collecting hobby.

Coin Prices at Wholesale

One of the finest methods to get ready to compete with the savvy coin dealer is to learn the wholesale pricing he pays for his coins. The Coin Dealer Newsletter, printed on grey paper and distributed weekly, is a widely used standard in US coinage. This magazine, which provides wholesale prices for every major type of US coin and a commemorative coin, is subscribed to by most professional coin dealers. The "green sheet" includes pricing for mint sets, slabbed coins, and banknotes. It's critical to remember that we're talking about the wholesale market when discussing Grey Sheet pricing.

Two factors distinguish this market:

- Most deals are for bulk amounts; therefore, pricing does not refer to single coins.
- Deals are for small-scale service transactions.

You can't go to a coin dealer and expect him to pay Grey Sheet "bid" pricing since he needs to assess and grade your collection. However, the Grey Sheet ought to give you a good idea of what your coins are generally worth, preventing you from selling a $1,000 coin for $200.

How to Sell Your Coins

Selling your coins should be a fully controlled act. Using the tips mentioned before in this chapter and your knowledge of the coin, you should do your best to ensure the final transaction is advantageous to you.

More importantly, the Certified Acceptance Corporation (CAC) should also have your coins certified. This will give you more trustworthiness in the eye of the buyer, and it will help you avoid undergrading (which is a practice by which unethical sellers and grading specialists deliberately lower the grade of a seller's coin to buy it for a cheaper price).

In addition to this, it would be great if you attributed your coins. You can do this easily if you use the Numismatic Guaranty Company (NGC)'s attribution service.

If you are attending a show, make sure you present your coins in a good light and make your stand attractive to everyone. Also, getting at least three different bids from different dealers is generally advised, as this will help you combat too cheap offers.

These are, of course, some general tips. Remember that trustworthiness, professional grading, and certification can make your offer more valid in the eyes of potential buyers.

Sell your coins in a variety of ways. There is no "right" or "wrong" place to sell coins. You *do* want this place to help you target your audience, so you will likely want to pick those that are more niche.

For instance, selling your coins at a flea market might not be profitable because people there are not necessarily looking for coins (and thus, they will not know how to appreciate the value of a coin you're putting out for sale).

Where to sell them, then?

Here are some options to take into consideration:

- *To a dealer.* Most often, you will get a lower price from a dealer because they want to sell the coin forward (and make a profit in the process as well). At the same time, selling to a dealer can be the safest and fastest way. Moreover, if your dealer has provided you with a buy-back guarantee that's still valid, you might be able to receive from the market price of a coin.
- *To a coin shop.* Like in a dealer, coin shops can be disadvantageous because you will probably not get the best price for your coins here.
- *To a pawn shop.* Depending on the coin and its rarity, a pawn shop might be willing to buy it from you. Naturally, though, the price might be much lower than the market price because the pawn shop might have to pay for an appraisal and still profit from this deal.
- *To a coin show.* Unlike in the first three situations, a coin show will most likely give you better control over the price. Of course, you should not overprice or underprice your coins, but a specialized show will allow you to display your products to people who are directly interested in coin collecting.
- *Online.* There are many ways to sell your coins online. Generalist sites like eBay or Amazon will allow you to sell coins (either through auctions or through direct selling). Furthermore, there are also specialized online auction/ commerce sites that sell coins and other similar collectibles. It is probably better to try selling your coins on these specialized sites (for the same reason, you shouldn't sell coins at a flea market, but at a professional coin show, for example).

- **On forums and social media.** The Internet is large, so that you might find groups and forums interested in coin collecting. Be sure you are ready to provide potentially interested people with all the documentation behind your coin so that you attest to its veracity!

- **Smelters and refiners.** If you want to melt your coin for its precious metal, go to a smelter or refinery. This is recommended only when the coin itself does not pose much value (e.g., it is of a very low grade), but you still want to recover your investment (and make a profit) by melting its precious metal.

Meeting with peer collectors and selling your coins to them is also a perfectly valid option. However, remember to make sure you enact healthy boundaries, especially if you are very good friends with them (otherwise, you might end up selling the coin for a much smaller price just because you feel odd not offering a friend a discount).

How To Find A Local Coin Dealer

If you're looking for a local coin dealer near you, don't just pull out your smartphone and type in "coin dealers near me." If you're going to show him coins to determine what they are, how much they are worth, or sell some coins, a little bit of research will go a long way. Many people listed in search engines under "Coins" are pawnbrokers, junk bullion purchasers, jewelers, and others who do not collect or study rare coins. They buy your coins for a low price, usually for their bullion value. Almost always, this procedure will result in you being taken advantage of. Before driving to a coin dealer, take your time and do some research to protect yourself.

Find a Trustworthy and Knowledgeable Local Coin Dealer

To ensure that you're dealing with an expert coin dealer who is honest and ethical, you should first consult the Professional Numismatists Guild (PNG) database.

The PNG has very strict membership requirements. You want to ensure that you have recourse if something goes wrong, and you also want an expert dealer who your peers have evaluated for ethical behavior. These coin merchants have been thoroughly checked to ensure their honesty. They are knowledgeable about numismatics and rare coins. Their reputation is more important to them than making quick money off an unsuspecting consumer.

Other Resources for Locating Local Coin Dealers

If none of the preceding methods result in locating a local coin dealer, the Yellow Pages (but not the online version) is the next place to look. Read the advertisements in the physical book's "Coin Dealers" section. Many times, just looking at a dealer's advertisement will tell you whether or not he is a good choice. Advertisements that say, "We buy trash jewelry and bullion," are not a good option. Rather than simply wanting to acquire coins for scrap metal prices, you should advertise "Specializes in US Coins" or "Gold Coins" or reference specific coins.

Last-Ditch Efforts to Locate a Local Coin Dealer

If none of the preceding methods produce results in your area, broaden your search to include local newspapers or online local news outlets. The "Coins" area of the classified advertisements is always where individuals post their private purchases and sales of coins.

Call a handful of these people and strike up a conversation with them. In the classified advertising, there is always a "Coins" section where people can post private advertisements to purchase and sell coins. But beware: some of these men may also be immoral! If you must go this way, make sure you are well-prepared. Get a copy of the Red Book and check up your coins yourself, so you know what's precious, and don't let these folks "cherry-pick" you. Sell everything or nothing at all, and never sell anything if it doesn't seem right!

Mistakes to Avoid

Everyone makes mistakes. Sometimes, even the most experienced coin collectors are liable to make them, so don't be too harsh on yourself if you stumble and fall now and again. Mistakes are how we learn.

Having said that, occasionally you can gain knowledge from the errors of others. Here are a few of the most typical coin-collecting mistakes to avoid, for instance:

- *Impulsivity.* Buying coins on impulse is never a good idea because it makes you likely to make most (if not all) of the mistakes we will discuss below. Always think things through and follow an actual strategy when buying your coins. Also, take some time to understand your psychology as a coin collector. Sometimes opportunities might arise, and they might feel like they're the best thing in the world, but the truth is that it is likely that they are tapping into your fear of missing out. Take your time, analyze matters in all seriousness, and make a purchase only when you are certain you want to proceed.

- *Not researching enough.* DO make sure to run your research, don't rely on whatever the dealer tells you. Even if they are not necessarily lying to you, they might be attempting to sell you a coin that does not suit your goals, collection, or budget. Be thorough and ruthless with your research - it is one of the best ways to prevent a lot of fraud.

- ***Following random tips.*** Not everything that's on the Internet is true, and not every tip you see on TV is necessarily valuable. Follow tips of advice that have a realistic foundation (and which can be proved factually).

- ***Buying coins from TV ads.*** Most of the time, coins sold on TV are either downright counterfeit or severely overpriced. The TV dealer is not your friend, and they are not making you an offer you can't refuse - they are trying to take advantage of you most of the time.

- ***Falling into the trap of dead-end investments.*** Sometimes, sellers might advertise their coins as low-mintage or rare when, in fact, they are neither rare nor valuable. This is a dead-end investment because coins that are not rare are not likely to appreciate well over time (they might gain a little appreciation, but that is due mainly to inflation and other economic factors that have nothing to do with the value of the coin per se).

- ***Buying self-slabbed coins.*** Just because a coin is nicely slabbed and presented does not necessarily mean it's valuable. Many of eBay's coins look as if they were ultra-rare, but if you do your research, you will find that the vast majority are just overpriced (or counterfeit).

- ***Negligence.*** Make sure you know how to preserve and protect your coin collection. We will discuss this in the following chapter, but keeping your coins at home or trying to clean them can severely diminish their value.

- ***Buying from sellers who have not been vetted.*** ALWAYS double-check your dealer. They might claim to be excellent and to have a lot of experience, but if other collectors and associations do not vet them, what they are trying to do likely is sell you fake coins (or majorly overpriced ones).

- ***Not understanding the value of a coin.*** We have already talked about *what* exactly makes coins valuable. It takes time and experience to learn how to spot a very good deal, but if you follow the general ground rules explained in this book, you can make some pretty good investments.

- ***Not insuring your coins.*** Your coin collection is an investment in the fullest sense of the word, and you want to be protected in case something happens. Insurance might be an extra cost to your hobby, but it is one of the best ways to ensure that your coin collection will be covered if something unpredictable happens.

Of course, these are not *all* the mistakes you can make–they are just the most common ones. There is a good chance that you will still make some mistakes in the beginning, but the tips in this subsection will help you stay away from those that might put you back by a lot.

Websites for Coin Collectors and Enthusiasts

The Internet is a fantastic resource for learning about coins and coin collecting. Regrettably, the Internet is also the world's foremost disseminator of disinformation. These top websites for information on coins were selected based on the accuracy and reliability of the data they offer. Furthermore, you can select from various sites that will provide you with the most diverse range of information and expertise.

<u>The United States Mint</u>

Category: Research, Coin Sales, and Auctions

You can get all the information you need about US coins on the United States Mint website and buy them there. The website is separated into three sections: commerce, history/learning, and news. The purchasing section contains all of the mint goods that are currently available. Typically, you may only buy coins and medals currently being manufactured at the mint.

PCGS Coin Facts

Category: Information, Research, and Coin Values

One of the most extensive websites is PCGS Coin Facts, which has information on almost every US coin ever produced. In-depth information is also provided on United States Mint design coins as well as private and territory issues, colonial issues, and private issues. The homepage has links to every sort of currency, making it simple to explore the site. By clicking on one of the coin type headings, you will be sent an overview of that coin kind.

Newman Numismatic Portal

Category: Information, Research, and Coin Values

One of the best coin collectors in the world, Eric P. Newman, donated to create the Newman Numismatic Portal. Newman's fascination with coins and voracious curiosity propelled him to become one of coin collecting's most illustrious scholars. Newman began selling his coin collection in 2013. The proceeds from his selling totaled millions of dollars. A portion of this sum was used to launch the Washington University in St. Louis, Missouri, numismatic research portal. The Newman Numismatic Portal provides something for everyone, whether you're just starting out or are an experienced collector.

Coin News.net

Category: News and Blogs

The Coin News website contains numismatic articles and coin-collecting pricing calculators. This is one of the best new coin-collecting websites in the business. The site is updated regularly with breaking news and current coin collector information. This website includes coin news from the United States Mint, other international mints, news affecting bullion prices, coin exhibitions, and auctions.

NGC World Price Guide

Category: Information, Research, and Coin Values

One of the most reputable coin price guides in the world is the NGC Global Pricing Guide. The world coinage from 1600 to the present is included in this fully searchable database of coin prices. This comprehensive collection of world coin values was prepared in collaboration with NGC and Krause Publications' NumisMaster. The information, which includes coin values, images, and specifics like weight, composition, bullion value, artist/engraver, and edge type, is arranged using Krause-Mishler catalog numbers. Access to the data is free for all users.

PCGS, www.pcgs.com

Category: Information, Research, Buying/Selling, and Coin Values

Heritage Auctions is the world's biggest numismatic auctioneer in Dallas, Texas. Heritage also maintains offices in the United States, Europe, and Asia. Heritage, founded in 1976, offers a diverse selection of US and international coins, rare cash, fine and decorative art, sports memorabilia, and various other excellent collectibles. Although Heritage is the largest supplier of rare and precious coins and cash, the typical collector may still add to their collection with less expensive items.

Great Collections Inc.

Category: Buying/Selling, Information, and Coin Values

In order to serve the rare coin and bullion sectors, Ian Russell founded Great Collections as a new coin auction company in 2010. His extensive knowledge of Tele-Trade coin auctions enabled him to develop an online coin auction business that caters to both beginning and experienced coin collectors.

Mint Error News

Category: News & Blogs

Mint Error News is the website to visit if you are interested in mint errors. Mike Byers is the president and editor/publisher of Mike Byers Inc. He has been a professional numismatist for over 35 years and is a world authority on mistake coins. The free and fully downloadable Mint Error News Magazine is the website's feature. Each issue contains full-color images, discoveries, and in-depth instructional content for error coin collectors.

American Numismatic Association

Category: Coin Clubs and Interaction with Others

The largest coin club in the world has a fully updated and contemporary website to help you with your coin-collecting journey. The American Numismatic Association (ANA) was established in 1891 by five individuals who enjoyed the hobby of coin collecting. More than 125 years later, the ANA maintains one of the most extensive Internet presences, offering information to assist coin collectors worldwide.

The ANA provides something for every coin collector, from contacting a coin dealer or coin club to attending an informative conference. It includes unique tools and information, virtual tours of the ANA Money Museum, and materials for young collectors. The monthly publication of the ANA, The Numismatist, is available for download if you are a member.

Kitco Bullion Prices

Category: Information, Research, and Coin Values

Many coins are constructed of precious metals, which significantly impact the coin's value. The price of precious metals can change dramatically under unpredictable market conditions. As a result, a coin may be valued more as bullion than as a collectible coin on the open market. If you want to purchase bullion coins, this website will provide you with historical and current spot prices for gold, silver, platinum, palladium, and rhodium.

Coin Collecting as Investment

You may be interested in coin collecting as an investment opportunity. This does not take away anything from what coin collecting is, as even serious collectors still have profit in the back of their minds. There is an ongoing trend where financial advisers encourage their clients to keep 10% of their investments in precious or rare coins with high numismatic value. Their advice: "Buy the highest quality, rarest coins you can afford."

If you are considering such an investment, you can go directly to the US Mint, where you can purchase US Coins or World Coins.

Coin collecting is slowly spreading around the world. The hobby has matured in the US and Canada, and you can find many clubs catering to it. They have the means to spread and perpetuate it to make sure that coin collecting will continue in the years to come.

Elsewhere in the world, like in Australia and some European countries, the hobby is fast gaining followers and has a potential for a wider and more vigorous coin-collecting community owing to their fast-growing economy and long coinage history. People there are beginning to take note of the prospective value of these coins and are taking steps to buy them cheaply.

Book 3: Rarest Coins

There are various categories that coins can fit into (such as the material used for making them, for example, or the event in which they were created). To make it easier for you, we won't delve too far into the precise classifications and will instead give you an overview of the basic coin types.

Main Types of Coins

<u>Gold Coins</u>

Gold coins were first made during the time of King Croesus of Lydia around 560 B.C. They were not made of pure gold but from a natural alloy of silver and gold called electrum. Pure gold and silver were used later and then spread to many civilizations, including the Greek and Roman empires and throughout Europe.

Gold has always been an attractive investment, and with the price of gold at record highs, it has become more so. Investors generally think of gold bars when they invest, but gold coins have other benefits like viability as currency and being in small denominations.

Gold coins generally cost a little more than the worth of their gold content because of an additional 4 to 8 percent premium to cover minting and distribution costs. But despite this, gold coins are still more valuable because they are easier to sell and manage than gold bars. If a US monetary system breakdown, gold coins can still be used as currency.

In a bull market, according to the American Gold Exchange, modern gold bullion coins are not likely to gain as much value as rare and collectible gold coins because they are not minted in limited numbers.

It is always best to keep gold in a bank-safe deposit box, but you can also keep your coins at home. Beware of the dangers of this practice, like the possibility of theft or fire damage. Gold is a soft metal, so one has to be careful when handling gold coins, as they can easily be scratched or dented. Damage can lower their cost and value.

The two main types of gold coins are:

- **Bullion coins** – refer to coins whose value comes from the worth of the metal rather than from its face value. They are priced and sold according to the gold's weight in the coin, with the additional premium. Examples are the US Eagle coin, the Canadian Maple Leaf coin, and the South African
Krugerrand.
- **Collectible coins** – also known as "numismatic" coins. These are gold coins whose price is based on their rarity, age, and condition rather than their weight in gold. Collectors appreciate their beauty, historical significance, and, of course, potential investment value.

Silver Coins

1895 Morgan Silver Dollar

Because silver prices have increased, silver coins are only issued now as commemorative or silver bullion coins. Before 1967, coins in the US and Canada had silver content in circulated coins.

The following factors influence the price and value of silver coins:

- The rarity of the silver coin
- Percent of Purity/Finesse
- Grade or Quality
- Bullion market value of silver as a commodity.

An excellent example of a silver coin worth investing in is the Morgan Silver Dollar, one of the country's most collected coins. It is a work of art and has great historical significance. Collectors love its beauty and affordability. Morgans are some of the rarest and most sought-after US coins ever minted.

Commemorative Coins

In the 1930s, when the US Mint was required by law to produce commemorative coins, they first gained popularity in the US. They were sold to distributors who added a premium price to the coin's value. This, however, was short-lived as collectors began to complain about speculators manipulating the market and pricing. The US Mint began to produce fewer commemorative coins as a result.

Much like they do today, the first wave of commemorative coins attracted a lot of individuals to coin collecting. Commemorative coins continue to be attractive and beautiful, both to collectors and to those with little interest in coin collecting.

Revolutionary Coins

In brief, revolutionary coins were in circulation throughout that time (such as the American Revolution of 1776). These coins can be fairly expensive due to their historical significance (but this depends on other factors too).

Ancient Coins

Sometimes people confuse ancient coins with gold or silver coinage. This may not always be the case, though, as old coins were produced using different materials (such as glass, ivory, or porcelain, for example).

A further misunderstanding regarding ancient coins is that they are prohibitively pricey. This may be the case in some circumstances, but you can still own one (or more) without going broke because a coin's market value is not solely based on its age.

Souvenir Pennies

It's interesting to see these coins. They are regular coins that have been altered through pressing, lengthening, and design. The most intriguing thing about them is that, with the exception of these commemorative pennies, it is forbidden to mutilate them in order to put them back into circulation. Unusual documentation for any collector's files!

Medallions

Various coins are frequently referred to as "medallions" (including commemorative ones). Generally speaking, "medallions" are any kind of round, ornamented piece of metal with some sort of significance (such as monetary value, for example). Actual medallions, however, typically don't have a legal tender associated with them.

Tokens

Trade tokens are frequently quite uncommon and collectible. They may occasionally be worth several hundred dollars (e.g., Civil War tokens, for example). When people were having financial difficulties and needed something for their currency but silver and gold were in short supply, these tokens were frequently produced.

At face value, tokens were often worth $1 or less, while some can be worth, for instance, $5. They were utilized in regular transactions just like "standard" circulation coins.

Error Coins

These coins were made incorrectly (such as a double denomination, overdate, or brokerage). Some could be tempted to think they are worthless because they are fresh from the mint. However, depending on the flaw and the time period, mistake coins can also be highly expensive.

Silver Certificates

To exchange one silver dollar, people utilized outdated silver certificates. However, the government stopped producing these certificates in 1964, at which point they lost their validity. A certain amount of silver could be exchanged for silver certificates for a certain period of time, though, and this eventually led to a new coin-collecting craze as everyone "suddenly" started seeking for these.

Art Bars

Art bars, a peculiarity, were particularly well-liked in the 1970s. They were one-ounce, thin, rectangular silver bars with polished surfaces and engraved designs honoring just about anything you can think of, from your wedding to your kitten.

Art bars were sought for at initially because mintages were few. But as more and more of these art bars crowded the market, patrons gradually grew weary of it. Art bars attracted a lot of collectors to the world of coins, just like the other coin varieties on our list that started a new trend.

There isn't a certain correct or wrong coin to collect. Sure, some coins are worth more than others today, but in the end, the value depends on a variety of circumstances rather than just the coin's type.

Special Coins

Special coins may end up as priceless heirlooms, a story passed down through the years, or a sought-after object to sell in the future. A coin may be special for several different reasons, and it may symbolize different things to different people.

The country of their birth or the country of their ancestors may have been the coin's place of origin. A specific coin, like a sixpence found in a Christmas pudding or given to a woman on her wedding day, may have been handed down through a family for many years. Other than the coin holder and their kin, these coins might not have any special value.

Touch Pieces

When a well-known individual touches a coin, the area of interest grows and the coin gains value. In popular mythology, some coins that are supposed to have belonged to kings or famous historical figures possess special powers. These particular coins are referred to as "touch pieces," and they promise to heal the sick just by being touched.

One of the most well-known examples of a touch piece is Maundy Money. Collectors prize these special coins since they are a part of the Royal Family's annual custom in the UK.

Collectible Coins

Other coins have a particular place in the hearts of coin collectors. These collectors are known as numismatists.

Numismatists continually look for special or unique examples of coins and typically have relatively narrow interests. Another factor that makes certain coins special is their scarcity. Coins can become rare as they age; the rigors of time can wear a coin down, and coins have been occasionally recalled and melted down and re-struck.

This often occurs when precious metal coins are melted down for their metal content. These coins were originally worth their face value or denomination, but they have become much more valuable due to their rarity.

One rare coin is the gold Edward III Florin, the 'double Leopard.' Only three versions of this coin are now known to exist. It was first minted in 1344 and discontinued after just a few months. Two are in the hands of British museums, while the third was sold in 2006 for £680,000.

Proofs and Limited Editions

Some coins, which are not commonly used as currency, are intentionally designed to be scarce. These are proof and special edition coins with low-issue numbers intended solely for investors and numismatists. Mints immediately sell these pristine coins for more than their face value.

Proof coins were the first in history to be produced. They were meticulously struck before going into full-scale production to evaluate the quality of the dies. On the other hand, proofs are unique coins that are struck to a higher standard than regular coins and then handled with extreme care. Some are immediately sealed in capsules after minting to preserve their mint condition.

Setting low-issue limits ahead of time can benefit both mints and purchasers. It provides the buyer with an exclusive opportunity and guarantees early sales of the mint at a premium price. The maximum number of coins that can be struck is known as the issue limit, which is set before minting begins. The total number of coins struck or mintage may fall short of the issue limit. The mintage figure, however, cannot exceed the mint's issue limit.

In 2009, the Royal Mint issued a very low mintage of only 210,000 50p pieces for common circulation, another example of rarity contributing to a coin's uniqueness. The Kew Gardens 50p coin was minted to commemorate Kew Gardens, and due to its limited mintage, it is extremely rare. They're now worth far more than £100!

The Peter Rabbit coin is another popular 50p. It was published in 2016 to commemorate Beatrix Potter's 150th birthday. Some of the pieces sold for more than £800.

Bullion Coins

Investors primarily driven by financial objectives are another type of coin purchaser for whom coins can be special. They are looking for semi-numismatic bullion coins with both financial and collectible potential. This might include bullion coins minted in limited quantities as part of collectible series such as the Lunar or Queen's Beasts.

Gold bullion coins are taxed differently from gold bullion bars of the same weight. They are popular among investors as well as numismatists.

Coin Grading

What is the best method for grading coins?

Coin experts or numismatists use the term "grade" to describe the appearance of a coin. When one coin collector tells another that he has an uncirculated Charlotte 50 half-eagle, the latter is more likely to believe him. Assuming both collectors know the coin's grade, they should have a good idea of how it looks.

Because it can be arbitrary or biased, some people contend that determining a grade to rank or categorize a coin is more of an art than a science. This is particularly true when dealing with "Mint State" coins, where even small variations in grade can have a big impact on price. On the other hand, grading can be learned, researched, and applied to produce predictable and recognized results based on judgment rather than sensations. The best way to learn and understand coin grading, as with any language, sport, science, or research, is to study and practice one element simultaneously. While some people complain about "too many grades," professional coin graders recognize and appreciate the fact that there is a wide range of attributes between ranges.

- **Strike**: Tracing or scribbling a drawing or a sign onto a blank surface is what this method entails. A coin's strike can be mild or strong, depending on its design. The "Type II gold dollar" is an example of this, with the greatest strike and perfect alignment on both sides (obverse and reverse). As a result, these styles require weak strikes.

  Unless a coin is part of a series whose value is linked to a strike, the strike is not an important factor in determining the coin's grade.

- **Surface Area Conservation on the Coin**: The number and location of coin markings are essential in determining the grade. While there is no standard procedure for determining the number of coin markings that determine a coin's grade, there are several regulatory parameters for the significance of a scratch's area or location.

  For example, a coin with a deep scratch on the reverse will not be penalized harshly. However, if the identical scratch were made on a conspicuous or noticeable key point on the front, such as the Statue of Liberty's cheek, it would be penalized far more severely.

- **Luster vs. Patina**: Depending on the design, metal used, and "mint of origin," a coin's surface can have various textures, including satiny, prooflike, wintry, and semi-prooflike. When grading a coin, two factors must be considered: the amount of original skin that remains intact and the location and number of marks. Determine whether a coin is circulated or uncirculated by looking at its luster. A coin in Mint State has no abrasion or wear, and its luster should be free of significant fractures.

- **Color**: This is a somewhat subjective aspect of coin grading. One collector may find a "gold coin" with a dark green-gold coloring unattractive, yet another may find it desirable. Gold is less susceptible to color change than copper or silver because it is a relatively inert metal. Nonetheless, full-scale colors may be found in gold coins. Almost all US gold coins have been dipped or cleaned, and as a result, their original tint has been lost. Coin collectors gain experience and are drawn to coins that retain their original color. In many coin series, the first coin pieces are nearly impossible to find.

- *Attraction or Eye Appeal*: "Eye appeal" is defined by marks such as strike, shine, color, and surface area. Remember that a coin with high "eye appeal" may be strong in one quality but lacking in another, such as hue. Understanding how to grade a coin is critical for determining the value or price of a coin that one is buying or selling. So, if you're new to coin collecting, seek the advice of a seasoned collector before buying or selling your coins.

When you first start collecting nickels, you'll notice that some are worn out while others appear brand new. As one might expect, the condition of a coin influences its value. So, to calculate the value, we need a reference point.

The "Red Book" provides general values for each coin type based on a condition defined for each coin series. The Red Book illustration below depicts the grades or conditions of the Jefferson Nickel, which is very useful for beginners. It can be used to determine the condition of the nickels you find.

A standard has been devised to assist us in determining the condition or grade. A numeric value is assigned to coins on a 70-point grading system. It's known as the "Sheldon Scale."

The Sheldon Scale offers grades from Poor (P-1) to Mint State Perfect (MS-70.) Grades are typically assigned at significant locations along this scale, with the following being the most common:

Coin Grading Scale
Washington Quarters

AG 3   G 6   VG 10   F 12   VF 20

VF 35   XF 45   AU 55   MS 63   MS 69

- *Poor (P-1):* Identifiable only by date and mintmark; otherwise, it's a shambles.
- *Fair (FR-2):* Nearly smooth, but without poor coin damage.

- **Good (G-4):** Inscriptions have faded to the point where they blend into the rims in some spots; details are mostly removed.

- **Very Good (VG-8):** A little weathered, but all primary design elements are faintly visible. There isn't much in the way of core detail.

- **Fine (F-12):** The item is worn, yet the wear is even, and the overall design details are prominent. Rims are almost entirely separated.

- **Very Fine (VF-20):** - Moderately weathered, although with finer details. If present, the word LIBERTY should be legible in its entirety. Rims that are full and clean.

- **Extremely Fine (EF-40):** Lightly used; all devices are visible, with the primary ones being bold.

- **Uncirculated (AU-50):** Slight evidence of wear on high points; contact markings possible; little eye appeal.

- **Very Selective (AU-58):** The tiniest traces of wear, no major contact marks, nearly full shine, and good eye appeal.

- **Mint State Basal (MS-60):** Strictly uncirculated, an unattractive coin with no sheen, visible contact marks, and so on.

- **Acceptable Mint State (MS-63):** Uncirculated, but with touch marks and nicks, a slightly reduced shine, and a generally pleasing appearance. The strike is fair to the poor.

- **Mint State Choice (MS-65):** Uncirculated with a bright luster, few contact marks, and great eye appeal. The strike rate is higher than usual.

- **Mint State Premium Quality (MS-68):** Uncirculated with exceptional eye appeal, flawless brilliance, and no visible contact marks to the naked eye. Uncirculated with perfect luster, no visible contact markings to the naked eye, and exceptional eye appeal. The strike is beautiful and crisp.

- **Mint State All-But-Perfect (MS-69):** Uncirculated with perfect luster, sharp, attractive strike, and extraordinary eye appeal. This coin is flawless except for minuscule imperfections (at 8x magnification) in the planchet, striking, or contact markings.

- **Mint State Perfect (MS-70):** This is the perfect coin. The strike is sharp, centered, and on a new planchet, with no minute imperfections discernible at 8x magnification. The luster is bright, rich, and one-of-a-kind, with great eye appeal.

A more straightforward version might be useful: grading companies frequently certify valuable coins worth $100 or more. Certified coins sell for much more than uncertified coins because they reassure both the seller and the buyer that they are genuine. Buying certified coins ensure that we get what we pay for. However, there are a few confirmed forgeries out there.

Let's look at some nickels and see their grade or condition. In the Red Book description for a VG-8 Very Good coin, the second pillar from the right is practically gone, as with the piece below. The remaining three pillars are visible but worn, indicating that this piece is very good to fine. According to the Red Book, an AU-50 coin that is nearly uncirculated shows signs of mild wear only on the design's high points. Only half of the mint luster is still present. Take note of the flawless brilliance.

Book 4: Avoiding Fake Coins

Defective & Counterfeit Coins

Counterfeit and altered coins are more than a bother; they are fraudulent coins that detract from the hobby of coin collecting. They betray our faith in the coins and one another, and they detract from the enjoyment of the pastime.

Customers lose tens of thousands of dollars each year when they unknowingly purchase counterfeit or altered coins. Every day, someone in the United States unknowingly purchases a counterfeit coin. Unfortunately, the person who sold the coin is frequently unaware that it is a counterfeit or tampered coin. Federal legislation makes it illegal to duplicate or alter a genuine coin to increase its numismatic value. This, however, does not deter low-level criminals from producing thousands of counterfeit and altered coins each year. Many websites sell counterfeit coins in almost every denomination issued by the US Mint. Most of these sites are in Asia, where copyright, patents, and trademarks are routinely ignored and violated. Although the central government is aware of the situation, few actions are in place to deter violators. You are responsible for comprehending the coin you buy and protecting your investment.

What Exactly is a Forgery Coin?

What exactly is a tampered-with coin?

A fake coin is designed to resemble a real coin. An altered coin is a regular coin that has been altered by adding and removing metal to resemble a rare or expensive numismatic coin. Crooks' ability to create counterfeit coins has improved over time. The manufacturing procedures used to create counterfeit coins have evolved as technology has advanced. In one case, counterfeit coins are minted the same way as genuine ones.

The counterfeiters are brave enough, or stupid enough, to photograph and post their minting operation on the internet. The problem is not limited to high-value numismatic coins. Any coin of significant value has been forged.

They were of such excellent quality that even coin experts were duped when they first saw them. Counterfeiters have targeted coins ranging from a dime to a $20 Double Eagle gold coin. So, how can you safeguard yourself, your money, and your pastime?

Fortunately, counterfeit coin detection technologies are readily available and simple to use. The best tools to utilize are, for the most part, your eyes and your brain.

Ways to Spot a Fake Coin

Counterfeit coins are not a new phenomenon in coin collecting; they have existed for ages (if not millennia). Here are a few simple tactics and resources that can assist you in avoiding being misled by an unethical coin dealer or collector into accidentally acquiring a counterfeit coin. This essay will discuss simple methods for determining whether your coins are real or counterfeit. The methods provided here are not failsafe, but they can aid in identifying more blatant counterfeit coins.

Magnetic Slide Test

Another test you may do to detect counterfeit silver with magnets is a magnetic slide. This is a fun technique to discover fakes without any rigorous testing rapidly. It is simple to develop.

How it works: Silver has a property known as diamagnetism despite not being magnetic. Silver repels magnetic fields when it comes into contact with them. As a result, genuine silver going down a magnetic slide moves slower than false silver. A forgery will go down the slide with little resistance.

Look for the Seam

Counterfeit coins frequently contain casting seams that are visible to the human eye. Fake coins frequently include hole marks. Furthermore, many coins contain elaborate patterns or textures unique to that denomination and its series. If something doesn't feel right, it's preferable to look elsewhere.

Pay Close Attention to Markings

Many times, counterfeit coins may not have all of the same mintmarks as genuine coins. In this case, be certain to do as much research as possible on the frequent markings and designs that are consistent with the piece you are thinking about purchasing. If specific markings on the gold or silver coin you are about to acquire do not match up, ask if the vendor has the paperwork to back up their claim that the piece is genuine.

Find the Relief

Counterfeiters struggle to get the relief of a coin just perfectly. Typically, they are either far too high or far too low. A potential buyer can verify a coin's validity by stacking it with others from the same series. If the stack collapses, you have cause to be extra careful with the transaction.

Opposites Attract

Magnets do not attract elements such as gold and silver. As a result, if a magnet is cozying up to the newest addition to your coin collection, it is likely a forgery.

Determine the Weight of the Coin

Many counterfeit coins do not weigh the right amount, and weighing a coin is a simple way to verify if it was struck on an alloy-incompatible planchet (or blank). Weight measurement and comparison to weights are provided in A Guide Book to United States Coins (usually referred to as the Red Book); this will provide essential information to assist you in evaluating the coin's legitimacy. If the coin does not weigh the correct amount, it is likely counterfeit.

Measure the Diameter of the Coin

The diameter of counterfeit coins may be off, proving they are not real. A Vernier Caliper is a simple tool for measuring coin diameters to +/- 0.1 mm. The exact diameter, like the correct weight, is not a guarantee that the coin is genuine, but it is a useful data point to help you determine if it is genuine. This measuring device is made of plastic and costs less than $10.00.

Profit could be associated with forgery. It could be the counterfeiting syndicate's primary goal. The federal government frequently uses forgery for political purposes, such as during World War II. The Germans printed many British and American banknotes, intending to profit from them and destabilize the opponent's financial situation.

Replica coins are another well-known type of fake coin. The term "replica" means that the original coins have been duplicated with identical functions and markings. Nonetheless, common counterfeit coins have distinguishing features that professionals can identify. Some coin designs include the word "copy" on both sides. Most of these replicas are used as exhibits in museums and for educational purposes.

There are rumors that the Lebanese connection produces a lot of fake coins. It was found that these coins had been used to dupe numerous museums, businessmen, collectors, and other nations hunting for their lost ancient coinage.

The circulated intended forgery and the collector intended forgery are two types of forgeries in which the coin value is intended as a token, and the face values are accepted despite their illegality and intrusive, unimportant values.

If you want to be certain whether a coin is genuine or not, you should consult a professional. An experienced person with years of experience in this field could quickly identify the incorrect metal used for counterfeiting. If the person is a collector of such items, he should be more familiar with these coins. A collector should be more concerned about rare collectible coins because this is where counterfeiters profit. They target the most valuable market where they can make money.

Use Your Instincts

Suppose anything about a coin looks and feels odd, whether the surface or the color. It's probably a fake. Alloys are used to make many counterfeit gold coins. These are a different color than gold coins and seem to be made of brass. These metal pieces are often cast from molds and do not have the same smooth surface as a minted coin.

The noticeable color contrast, as well as the sand-cast surface, can be seen here. Also, the coin on the left is 12% lighter than on the right.

Notice the Details

On rare occasions, a counterfeit coin is made from the same precious metal as the original coin it is trying to replicate. This is particularly true with gold coins from the United States. We must compare the details from the coin's strike to a certified one. Occasionally, die markers on recognized counterfeits reveal the coin's actual origin. There may also be a lack of design depth and details missed. You can best protect yourself against even the cleverest counterfeiters by studying the details of coins and consistently handling certified pieces.

These two coins' dimensions, weight, and gold content are identical. The coin on the left lacks attention to detail and depth seen in the coin on the right.

The inscription on the edge of the left coin, as shown above, is one of the most telling signs that it is fake. The bottom coin in this picture is fake.

The best way to detect counterfeit is to be armed with information about the coins you intend to buy. You need to find out the actual weight and measurements of the real coin and compare it with the suspected counterfeit. Any significant differences should indicate that you have a fake in your hands.

Counterfeit items are typically lighter than genuine items, are too thick, or are made of the incorrect material. With experience as a coin collector, you will undoubtedly be able to identify counterfeits by their appearance, feel, and sound.

There are several factors to consider when determining whether a coin is genuine or counterfeit.

To identify verified coins, a coin restrike could be used. These coins are older than those first issued by the country with the same or specific features as the original coins.

One nation would sometimes copy the coins of another nation in ancient times. An individual may believe it is a forgery; however, it is not because they would have been legally authorized in the country from which they came.

Profit could be associated with forgery. It could be the counterfeiting syndicate's primary goal. The federal government frequently uses forgery for political purposes, such as during World War II. The Germans printed many British and American banknotes, intending to profit from them and destabilize the opponent's financial situation.

Replica coins are another well-known type of fake coin. The term "replica" means that the original coins have been duplicated with identical functions and markings. Nonetheless, common counterfeit coins have distinguishing features that professionals can identify. Some coin designs include the word "copy" on both sides. Most of these reproductions are utilized as exhibits in museums and for educational purposes.

There are rumors that the Lebanese connection produces a lot of fake coins. It was found that these coins had been used to dupe numerous museums, businessmen, collectors, and other nations hunting for their lost ancient coinage.

The coin value is intended to be used as a token in the circulated intended forgery and the collector intended forgery, and the face values are accepted in spite of their illegality and intrusive, inconsequential values.

If you want to be sure if a coin is fake or not, you should consider seeing a professional. An experienced individual with years of experience in this sector could quickly find the incorrect metal utilized for counterfeiting. If the person collects such things, he should be better knowledgeable about these coins. Because rare collectible coins are where counterfeiters make their money, a collector needs to be more concerned about them. They go for a precious market where they can make money.

Tips on How to Stay Away from Scams

Many people delight in shopping on the web, where fantastic coins can be discovered. An individual might do his shopping while at home because it is hassle-free and time-saving instead of searching for shops that offer collectible coins and other keepsakes.

An individual can distinguish a live auction from those on the Web since live auctions entertain bidders and call for the greatest price when the time comes. Many people bidding on the web make their experience so enjoyable, and they are familiar with the techniques on how they would win a web auction.

There are online websites where individuals can purchase any product that might interest them. This is where many coin collectors buy their preferred coins. They by browsing and discovering the product they desire

Even though it could be too risky to rely on a seller who is unidentified to the purchaser, many individuals are still making deals and payments via this sort of online auction.

Fraud is usually frequent nowadays, though numerous internet sites that do business online claim that the danger of fraud is not a thing to stress over. They state that just 0.0025 percent of real instances of fraud occur online. That implies only that one out of 40,000 noted web deals might be a fraud. On the other hand, the FBI has investigations showing that the figures are incorrect. According to their stats, they claim that fraud's danger is much greater.

An individual ought to trust the FBI for this protection. Even though one can state that most online coin selling is truthful and reliable, the procedure in which the deal is made could be most likely doubtful and unpredictable. There are business deals that are directly carrying out fraud. Aside from flea market dealers, in-person auctions, mail-order sellers, and some coin shops, the Web has the best odds of pulling off a fraud.

One protection a coin purchaser should be aware of is how to make "feedback." By doing this, an individual could see the scores of other bidders, and he might compare his deal with the deals of the others. If there is an excellent likelihood of fraud with negative feedback, the individual might withdraw his involvement in the auction.

An individual might get ideas by trying to find those members who have left "positive feedback" and compare it to the seller's response. An individual can evaluate what may be feasible helpful information from those responses. An individual should be cautious when it comes to any deal which is offered.

There are circumstances in which an individual is tricked into buying the product. The picture on the Internet showed the coin that individual wishes to have; however, they delivered something else entirely. These cases resemble fraud. An individual needs to ensure that the product he sees in the picture is the same product that will be shipped to him.

Here are some tips to help someone avoid fraud when conducting a coin search on the internet:

- An individual should save the online image of the coin he wishes to buy. Some sellers get rid of the title and the product image when a purchase has been made.
- An individual ought to get the auction information and the description. It could either be e-mailed to the individual or sent out by means of postal mail.
- If there are doubts concerning the auction, an individual should request an explanatory note. This will prevent misunderstanding and confusion on the part of the purchaser.
- An individual can decline any deal where he believes the price offered on the coin is too much. One ought to know the market price of the particular coin and contrast it to the price offered throughout the online transaction.

These are just a few pointers that guarantee an individual's safety when making online deals. Fraud could occur to anybody, specifically those interested in buying collectible coins online. It is essential to be informed and updated on the possibilities of coming across fraud.

Book 5: How to Protect Coins

How to Collect Coins

The collection of coins can be a funny, safe, and satisfying way of interacting with history and the world. Though it can be hard to differentiate common and cheap currencies from uncommon, undistributed money, there are patterns to make the procedure easier and less uncertain. Knowing where to get good coins, what to look out for in a purchase, and how to secure your coins will enable you to begin a collection easily.

Buying Coins

1. ***Visit any local coin shop around you:*** Although coin collecting is an extremely niche hobby, most cities have at least one coin shop close by. Such stores provide many coins at reasonable prices, making them a better place for prospective collectors. Many shop owners are collectors deep down and can aid in assessing the worth of singular coins, connecting with other sellers,

and finding prized, updated collecting possessions. Some coin shops buy coins straight from customers, while others purchase only from reliable retailers.

It would help if you were expectant that brokers would charge up to 20% more than single sellers:

2. **Go to coin sales and expos:** Although uncommon, local expos, coin auctions, and other dealings are better places for picking up new coins. Websites such as AuctionZip can enable you to discover upcoming auctions, whereas the American Numismatic Association preserves a list of future coin and currency expos on its website.

    Although eBay and other main marketplaces can produce better outcomes, it is almost difficult to check and confirm a coin's value before buying it. Instead, try specialized sites such as Heritage Auctions or Great Collections.

3. **Join a coin club:** In this short period, numismatic groups can be a better avenue for meeting fellow collectors, studying forthcoming events, and gaining instruction on how you can broaden your collection and knowledge. After a long time, club members who sell their coins usually give precedence and reduce prices to friends they've met through the organization.

    Organizations like the American Numismatic Association provide online directories linking you to local and regional clubs.

4. **Order from a national mint:** Most countries permit you to order memorial and specialty coins straight from the national mint. Although mints charge beyond face worth, they usually add value and genuineness to a guaranteed certificate. Mints also sell undistributed and resilient coins valued far more than their used counterparts.

Calculating Market Value

1. **Buy the book before you buy the coin:** A common numismatic saying explains that you should study a coin before you spend money buying it.
2. **Shun underpriced coins from qualified sellers:** When you see that a deal seems too good to be true, maybe it is. If a coin is undersold, inquire if it's authentic and hasn't been refined to hide errors. If you see it at a garage auction, flea market, or related organization, the seller

might not understand the real worth of their stock, but specialty collectors and sellers indeed do.

3. ***Study how coins are graded***: Coins are separately graded depending on the individual evaluator or country, but a place worthy of starting is the Authorized A.N.A. Grading System for United States Coins. At this point, coins are graded on a scale of 0 – 70, with additional points being provided to undistributed coins. Letters are included to denote the value, like the M.S. for Mint State or V.G. for "Very Good." In such a system, the coin with the maximum quality is listed as MS-70.

    Generally, U.S. evaluators are more knowledgeable than U.K. ones. Therefore, you should be conscious that a good coin in one country may be seen as defective in another.

    Several persons over-grade their coins to present them as market-friendly. To evade being swindled, ensure you double-check all the coins using a standard and authorized "by the book."

    Do not forget that categorizing, even by expert service, and grading standards can be altered from time to time.

4. ***Purchase a magnifying glass:*** Buy a reduced-powered and a high-driven magnifying glass for serious collectors. This will enable you to search for small signs and limitations of counterfeit, such as coins with improper fonts or askew optical elements. Watch out for sparkly coins, as particulars may have been smoothened away to look glossier.

5. ***Acquire a scale:*** A handy electronic scale is essential for coin collectors making costly purchases. Weighing a coin and relating it to collecting guides can assist you in recognizing counterfeits made from inexpensive materials. Furthermore, weighing a coin can enable you to determine its dissolving value or its worth when melted down into its raw materials.

Storing and Presenting Your Collection

1. ***Buy a safe to put your coins:*** For collectors, who are committed, buy water and a flame-resistant safe that can be locked to the ground. This will safeguard your investment from burglars, fires, and floods, something particularly essential while dealing with costly items. If you are collecting above all expensive or uncommon coins, improve to a safe-deposit box at a local post office or bank for added security.

If you have landowners insurance to insure your coins, keep an informed inventory with photographs to verify quality.

2. ***Evade great sunlight, temperatures, and humidity:*** Like most collectibles, you should keep your coins in a convenient, room-temperature atmosphere with little moisture. Avoid basement or loft rooms, places that are directly or indirectly exposed to humidity and sunlight; meanwhile, all have the possibility of damaging your coins.

3. ***Buy coin flips for separate coins:*** Coin flips are 2x2 holders commonly made of cardboard or vinyl. Comparable to trading or record card sleeves, they preserve your coin from the features while permitting you to present them. Avoid the polyvinyl (PVC) holders because they can destroy the coin over time, even engraving its surface.

4. ***Buy coin albums, folders, and boards for complete collections:*** As the flips, coin album sleeves comprise separate sections bound together on binder-sized sheets. Both separately and with a binder are available. Coin boards and folders are specialties, cardboard vessels having holes through which coins can be pushed into it. These are typically sold by form, with various folders for quarters, pennies, and the like.

How To Handle Your Coins Correctly

You can damage your coins with how you handle them. First, it is through contact with your skin, touching coins with your naked hands. You cannot see them, but as we mentioned, human skin secrets acids and oil. When you touch them with your naked fingers, you leave these deposits on their surface, which will eventually cause damage. Also, there is a way you should hold a coin. This is how you handle your coins:

- Hold it by the edges, between the thumb and forefinger, always. Never touch the face of the coin.
- Hold a coin over a soft place, just in case it falls, so it does not get scratched on a hard surface.

If you must clean a coin to remove dirt, use only mild soap and clean water, then pat it dry with a soft towel. However, experts advise collectors who want to keep the value of their coins to avoid cleaning and polishing them.

Improper coin cleaning to make them look shiny devalues them. If the coins do not have dirt that needs to be cleaned, try to keep them in the same condition you found them. An old coin with deep age coloration is far more desirable and valuable than a polished coin with the surface scratched to appear new.

Always handle your hands with cotton gloves, even if you've just washed them.

Collector coins should be handled carefully to avoid wear or introducing substances that could cause spots or color changes. Many holders provide adequate protection for normal handling but are cautious before removing a coin from its holder.

Only the edge of proof or uncirculated coin should be touched. Fingerprints alone have the potential to reduce the coin's grade and, thus, its value. When inspecting another person's coins, you must always handle them on edge regardless of grade. Picking up collectible coins by their edges will become second nature if you practice.

It is not a good idea to hold numismatic objects in front of your mouth. Small particles of moisture can cause spots.

When placing a coin outside a holder, place it on a clean, soft surface. A velvet pad is an ideal surface for handling valuable materials regularly. A clean, soft cloth or a blank piece of paper may suffice for less valuable items. There should be no dragging of coins across any surfaces.

Wear a clean white cloth or surgical gloves, as well as a mask, if you're handling a lot of circulated coins that are higher grade or highly valuable coins.

One of the most important rules for all coin collectors is to avoid causing wear or introducing substances that may cause spots or color changes. Avoid any direct human contact with your coins. This includes not handling the coins with your bare hands. Fingerprints are the sworn enemies of collectible coins. You should avoid allowing one coin to touch another because this can result in nicks and scratches. To avoid destroying them, take coins out of their storage containers only when necessary.

Uncirculated or Proof coins should be handled only on edge, as even a minor fingerprint can lower the grade and thus the value. Proof coins are equally valid as regular coins because they have been struck at least twice with polished dyes on an equally polished planchet.

The US government packages coins in uncirculated mint sets for sale to coin collectors. Picking up collectible coins by their edges while wearing clean white cotton or surgical gloves is best practice. A face mask is also recommended to prevent small moisture particles from causing unsightly spots. Never sneeze or cough near coins because this can leave marks on the coin and ruin it.

Coin holders provide adequate protection for everyday use. If you must remove the coin and place it outside the holder, ensure it is on a clean and soft surface, preferably a velvet pad. It is an ideal surface for handling valuable numismatic materials and a must-have. A clean, soft cloth can be used to clean lower-value coins. To avoid scratches, avoid dragging coins on any surface. Keep in mind that even wiping it with a soft cloth can cause scratches, lowering its value.

Many new collectors are unaware of this issue but understanding how to handle coins is critical. It is so important that it should not be an option but a requirement.

Mishandling coins can significantly reduce their quality and, thus, their value. You might think that touching the coin with your bare hands isn't a big deal, but your fingers can damage it, especially if done repeatedly.

How exactly should you handle the coins in your collection? Here are some tips:

- Never handle them with your bare hands - this is what your cotton gloves are for.
- If your coins are placed in a special holder, leave them in, don't try to pull them out.

- Always pick up your coins by the edges, using your thumb and forefinger. Do not hold coins by touching the front (obverse) or back (reverse) surface, as it can damage the finish's design and quality.
- If you are afraid you might drop your coin while handling it, hold it over a thick, soft towel.
- Avoid talking when you handle your coins. Those tiny, invisible droplets of saliva can create spots that are impossible to remove, as unbelievable as they might sound.

Your coins are not just "money." They are valuable artifacts of the past (and present). They mark significant historical moments back in the day, and more than that, they bear with them stories never to happen again. From the happy kid who bought an ice cream with his coin 70 years ago to the grandma who gave it to him, the collection of coins carries their hopes, pleasures, and sadness at the same time.

Treat them as such. Treat them like the works of art they are, with care, dedication, and attention!

How to Store Your Coins

To prevent scratching your coins and lowering their numismatic worth, you must preserve them carefully. Depending on the worth of the coin you are storing, you need to utilize the right kind of holder.

You can buy commercially available folders and albums to store your series or type collection. When using paper envelopes, be sure that their composition is ideal for holding coins, especially valuable coins, as sulfur or other chemicals in the paper can react with the coin's pigment and change its color.

Mylar and acetate-based plastic flips are excellent long-term storage materials, but because they are hard and brittle, they may scratch the coin if the coins are not carefully inserted and removed. "Soft" flips used to be made from polyvinyl chloride (PVC), which decomposed over time and gave disastrous results for the coins. PVC lent a green appearance to the coins. PVC flips are no longer produced and sold in the US.

Tubes can hold many same-size coins and are suitable for bulk storage of circulated coins and higher-grade coins if they are not moved. Use hard plastic holders for more pricey coins because they are non-toxic and can shield coins from dents and other physical harm.

For more valuable coins, slabs are an option because they offer effective protection. Slabs are hermetically sealed coin holders made of hard plastic. However, there are certain disadvantages, including the cost and the difficulty of accessing the currency in the event of a necessity.

Long-term storage requires a dry atmosphere with little temperature variation and low humidity. You should limit your exposure to wet air because it will lead to oxidation. While decreasing oxidation won't always lower the coin's value, it will make it appear more appealing. Placing silica gel packets in the coin storage area will help control ambient moisture.

Even if you keep your collection in a safety deposit box, you should still occasionally check on it. If not stored properly, issues could arise, but you can take action before any severe harm is done.

To properly care for your coins, you must store them because doing so will shield them from various factors that could harm them.

Unfortunately, no method can give complete security for your funds. However, you can pick the correct atmosphere and coin supplies to preserve your coins from harm while in storage.

Extremes such as a cellar (cold and damp) or attic (hot and harsh) must be avoided to maintain your coin collection in the best possible shape. The greatest place to put it is in a den or bedroom. Additionally, select a location away from the kitchen where cooking oils and moisture will not rapidly infiltrate your coin holders, folders, and albums. If you live near the water or sea, you must take extra steps to protect your coins from damage caused by the damp and salty climate. Copper coins are particularly vulnerable to environmental degradation caused by moisture and salt in the air in coastal areas.

A safe deposit box at a bank is one of the safest locations to keep your coin collection. Unfortunately, this is also the costliest option. Bank vaults are built to keep criminals and firefighters out. Bank vaults are composed of a substance that emits water vapor, which keeps the temperature in the vault low in the event of a fire. Over time, some water naturally escapes. As a result, your collection would be in a highly humid atmosphere. A silica gel pack inside your safe deposit box will absorb the water vapor. To keep it fresh and absorb as much water vapor as possible, change it at least twice a year.

Buying a safe for your home or business to store your coin collection is a less expensive choice. There is no recurring annual cost with a safe, as with a safe deposit box. Unfortunately, home and business safes are made of the same material as bank vaults. You should also use a silica gel pack to absorb humidity and protect your money from harm. You might also consider investing in a properly placed alarm system. This will safeguard your house, family, and currency collection from various hazards. Among the hazards are intruders, fire, flood, and dramatic weather fluctuations.

Because of the coatings, glue, and wood, wooden bookcases and cabinets can emit dangerous chemicals into the atmosphere around your coin collection as they age. A lockable metal cabinet will keep your collection safe because it does not have the problems with wood, even though it is not as secure as a safe. Metal tends to draw moisture in the form of condensation, so be careful where you place your metal cabinet. Taking humidity from the air and putting it on your coins might be disastrous. Protecting, conserving, and keeping your coin collection properly can ensure that future generations appreciate your coins.

To fully understand why it is essential to store your coins properly, you should consider the following causes of coin damage (all of which are more popular than you might think):

- *Humidity.* The single most common cause of damage when it comes to collectible coins. Both silver and copper create chemical reactions with moisture, which can be found everywhere. As such, it is quite challenging to reduce the risk (there are ways you can do this, but it is not 100% certain, so the more cautious you are with it, the better off you will be).

- **Extreme temperature.** Keeping your coins in areas that are too warm can increase moisture, air pollution, and acids (all of which can damage the coin faster than usual). Likewise, keeping your collection at very low temperatures can cause condensation on the surface of the coins.

- **Acids.** To damage them, you don't have to pour actual acids over your coins. Sometimes, coin holders and storage supplies are made from paper or cardboard, and the acids typically found in these materials can lead to the toning and tarnishing of the coins. As such, you must avoid any coin storage materials containing acids.

- **Chlorine.** This harsh chemical can corrode coins and lead to toning them. Again, you mustn't necessarily dip the coins in chlorine to see such effects. Sometimes plastic coin holders contain PVC, which includes chlorine in its composition. As such, it is essential only to use PVC-free coin holders.

- **Air pollution.** Not only is air pollution incredibly harmful to us humans, but it can also damage coins in time. Protect them by keeping them away from the outside air as much as possible (especially if you live in or around a metropolitan area).

- **Improper handling.** As mentioned before, you should be extremely careful handling your coins because this is a major source of damage for them.

OK, so taking all of these bits of information into account, where exactly should you store your coins? Some options include the following:

- Acid-free paper sleeves or envelopes, folders, tubes, albums, coin holders, or flips
- Small PVC-free plastic bags or "slabs" (sealed hard plastic) - you might want to use these for the more valuable coins

To avoid handling your coin storage, try to keep a catalog of all your coins. This will help you know exactly what coins you have and what coins are required to complete a series in your collection. You can keep your catalog in a good old-fashioned notebook or an app or software.

Let's say you have already picked your storage type. Where do you put your sleeves, envelopes, or slabs to make sure you protect your coins from even more potentially damaging factors?

Keep these tips in mind:

- Avoid humidity, high heat, low heat, acids, salt, chlorine, and air pollution (as per the tips we have already expanded on above)

- Make sure your storage place is dark, dry, and temperature-controlled
- Avoid the basement, as it can be very cold and humid in there
- Likewise, avoid the attic, as that can be too hot and too harsh
- Your bedroom or your den will most likely meet all criteria because you spend comfortable time there (and as such, it is likely that your coins will be "comfortable" as well)
- Preferably, use metal cabinets instead of wooden ones because they might be more protective against moisture. DO make sure you pay attention to where precisely you locate the metal cabinet as well, as it can still attract moisture if, for example, it is located right next to a moist wall.
- You can also buy specialized coin collection cabinets. Adding silica gel envelopes to these cabinets will help you maintain the moisture at optimum levels for your coins.
- Likewise, you can also store your coins in a safety deposit box or a home or office safe, as these places will most likely meet all the necessary criteria.
- If you think the collection will be observed very often, choose a storage method that will allow you to easily do this without pulling the coins out of the sleeve.

The more you can do for your coins, and the more probable they will survive the sands of time in a pristine state. As such, your investment will have even more value years from now when (or if) you decide to sell your collection.

Boxes, jars, and bags can be used to store fewer precious coins, but they are unsuitable for more costly coins. There are specially designed coin envelopes made of acid-free paper that contain individual coins and give a convenient, low-cost way to store most coins.

Plastic resealable bags or "flips" are an excellent alternative for coin storage since they allow you to see the coin without removing it from the cover. Similar to plastic flips, Mylar-lined cardboard sleeves (typically 2"x2") are an excellent way to store and package coins for transportation. Cardboard or plastic coin albums are ideal for storing a collection of coins associated with a specific nation or theme.

Tubes are plastic containers that are useful for storing a group of inexpensive coins of the same size. Very costly coins are frequently "slabbed" or encased in hard plastic carriers, which provide the best protection of any storage method.

A couple of things to bear in mind when it comes to storage: if you reside in a humid location, add some silica gel to your storage container and keep your coins in their storage containers in a secure place, such as a safe or fireproof box.

They should not be stored in a room with extreme temperatures, either too hot or too cold. Storage space/place must be cool and dry. Remember what humidity or moisture in any form can do to a coin? Thus, keep it cool, use a fan if you have to, and let it always be dry.

Only use original holders. They are made of quality material and do not contain PVC found in cheaper, softer holders. Always go for the quality.

A metal cabinet is preferable to a wood cabinet. You see, cabinets made from wood have coatings and adhesives that can damage your coins. A metal cabinet will work best here. However, it is important to ensure that the cabinet is within a place away from any possible contact with moisture. This means an adequately aired place as metal can experience condensation and attract moisture.

If you have high-value coins, you might want to put them in a safe deposit box in a bank or a safe in your home.

Coin Care and Cleaning

In most circumstances, it is not necessary to clean coins. While you might assume that bright coins seem better, collectors prefer coins that have their original appearance. Cleaning a coin can halve or perhaps more than halve its collector value.

Cleaning coins, like repairing works of art, is best left to professionals who understand when it's appropriate, which techniques will work best, and how to use them effectively.

If you must go to the trouble of cleaning coins, never use abrasive cleaners. Scrubbing the coin with a delicate cloth can also leave small but noticeable scratches, reducing the coin's value.

If a coin's surface appears tarnished, it is best to leave it alone. The color shift is caused by a natural process known to collectors as toning. Chemical reactions have occurred on the coin's surface, most commonly with sulfur compounds. It is impossible to stop the reaction.

" Dips " can be used to remove molecules from the surface. Dipping is an excellent example of a procedure that, if used at all, should be performed only by professionals. Natural toning can also increase the value of a coin.

Occasionally, dirt and other foreign substances stuck to a coin can be removed. You can soak the coin in olive oil or soapy water for a few days before thoroughly rinsing it with tap water. Allow the coin to dry naturally or with compressed air. Rubbing the coin is not permitted. Commercial coin cleaners can also be used to remove foreign substances quickly.

A coin that has been cleaned with an abrasive will have hairlines. Abrasive cleaning can also leave debris in the crevices of the coin.

If the coin has been dipped, it may or may not be detectable. An original coin may exist, but it's unlikely. Dipping can also be used to remove the luster from a coin.

Natural coins have a distinct appearance that reflects their storage history. The toning of haphazardly stored coins appears "dirty." Coins stored in a coin cabinet for a long time usually have beautiful colored toning.

Coins stored in a clean metal vault (such as an old-fashioned "piggy" bank) can last for a long time and remain white (or red). Coins in albums either develop "ring toning" or "one-sided toning," both of which are unappealing. Coins stored in mint bags frequently exhibit incredible rainbow toning, similar to that found in coin cabinets.

Clean copper, bronze, or brass coins have an artificial tint that resembles a toned gold coin. They're still uneven and have an unusual color, even after re-toning. The presence of red in the crevices of that VF copper coin is not a good sign. Natural-toned and circulated copper has a relatively uniform color, but it may be dark and dusty around the lettering and other protected areas. Uncirculated copper (particularly proofs) can have a very uneven tone, so don't dismiss such a coin out of hand.

On the other hand, silver coins that have been cleaned and re-toned are extremely color consistent, including the tops of inscriptions and protected areas. Silver coins with natural toning will usually show color variations in these locations. Be aware that a consistent slate grey hue on silver can be easily achieved using a variety of chemicals. Finally, a heavily toned and then dipped silver coin will have a grey appearance caused by surface roughness rather than tarnish. A close look with a bright magnifier will reveal this.

According to the ANA, rapid "hard-line" color changes do not occur on naturally toned coins. Naturally, toned coins exhibit a gradual change in hue or shade. In any case, the main thing is to examine a large number of coins and draw your conclusions. When purchasing coins for your collection, your point of view is the most crucial factor to consider.

While it is essential to keep your surroundings clean, it is best if you do not clean the coins at all. A shiny coin may look nice but keeping a collectible coin's original appearance is critical. Cleaning the coin can significantly reduce its numismatic value.

Unnecessary cleaning reduces the value and cost of collectible coins. The patina on a coin develops over time and is part of its essence and history, reflecting a value far greater than its face value. You can reduce its value by up to 90% by removing it! Collectors value coins with attractive patinas because they protect the coin's surface.

Cleaning coins, like any other work of art restoration, must be done by professionals. They know which techniques will work best while keeping the coin as valuable as ever.

STOP if you believe a recently discovered tarnished coin needs to be cleaned. It's not a good plan. It is preferable to ignore the coin. The color change you see is caused by a natural process known as toning. And, if allowed to progress naturally and produce pleasing results, it can sometimes increase the coin's value.

The chemical reactions of the atoms on the coin's surface, usually with sulfur compounds, cause toning. Although it cannot be reversed, "dips" that remove molecules from the coin's surface are available. However, keep in mind that professionals should only do this.

Contrary to popular belief, cleaning coins is not a normal and natural part of caring for a coin collection. The only time you should clean your coins is when you add circulated ones to your collection (and especially if you want this to be an activity you share with your kids).

In all other cases, you should avoid cleaning coins at all costs. Cleaning can cause significant damage to old or inherited coins. Even if the damage is minor, cleaning them can remove their aged appearance and reveal minor cracks and scratches in the metal.

If, however, you find yourself in the first situation and want to clean circulated coins, you can do so by following these tips:

- Make sure you have all your tools handy, namely two small plastic containers, a clean, soft towel, running tap water, rubbing alcohol (if you want to), and some mild dish detergent.
- Start by washing your hands with soap to remove the oils and fine grit from your fingers.
- Take your towel and lay it down, folded over a couple of times. Make sure it's close to the containers.
- Create a soapy bath in one of the containers, using mild dish soap and warm tap water. You should use a plastic container because glass, metal, or China can scratch your coins. Also, make sure not to overdo it on the dish soap - you don't want to give your coins a full bubble bath; you want to make sure you remove the potential viruses and bacteria from them.
- Pick the coin you want to wash with care and immerse it in soapy water. Gently rub both of its sizes between your fingers, moving from the edge of the coin to the center.
- Take it one by one, don't add all the coins you want to wash in the container, as they might damage each other.
- Run the washed coin under warm tap water until the soap residue is gone. Keep in mind that you should be as gentle as possible!
- Fill your other container with distilled water and swish the coin around. This will help remove chlorine residue or other contaminants that might hurt the coin's appeal.

- Set the towel aside to dry out on the towel. Before putting it away in your collection, ensure the coin is thoroughly dried. Also, as usual, remember only to handle it by the edges.

Cleaning Different Types of Coins

- *Uncirculated Coins* – These should never be cleaned because cleaning will ruin any mint luster.
- *Gold Coins* – These should be washed carefully in clean, warm soapy distilled water using a fluffy cotton washcloth or a very soft toothbrush. You should take extra care to avoid disfiguring or scratching gold.
- *Silver Coins* – Valuable silver coins should not be cleaned at all. The blue,-green, or violet oil-like tarnish, dirt, minerals, or other residues some silver coins have enhances their appearance and should be left alone. Dark silver coins must be cleaned with ammonia, rubbing alcohol, vinegar, or polish remover with acetone. Do not rub or polish them.
- *Copper Coins* – If necessary to clean, soak them in grape oil. If not available, olive oil will do. Never attempt to rub them in any way. However, getting results may take several weeks to a year, so be patient.
- *Nickel Coins* – These are best cleaned with warm, soapy distilled water using a soft toothbrush. If cleaning badly stained nickel coins, use ammonia diluted 3 to 1 with distilled water.

What To Avoid

- Do not use silver, metal, or even jewelry polish. They are too harsh for coins. They may leave little scratches on their surface.
- Never rub a coin, even if to remove a stain.
- Do not use tissue paper or paper towels to dry a coin.

Mint Coins

Coin holders provide enough protection for ordinary handling. If you must take the coin out and need to put it down outside the holder, make sure you place it on a clean and soft surface, preferably a velvet pad. It is an ideal surface and a must-have for handling valuable numismatic materials. A clean, soft cloth may be used for coins with lesser value. Avoid dragging coins on any surface to avoid scratches. Even wiping with a soft cloth can cause scratches that reduce its value.

There are several rules to follow when cleaning coins you have recently obtained, discovered, purchased, or inherited.

- Never clean a coin whose numismatic value you do not know. If you're unsure whether it's valuable or not, don't clean it. It is best to leave coins in their original state. It is preferable to err on the conservative side than to ruin the coin for nothing. Keep them in specially designed holders. Coin collectors and dealers prefer coins in their original state and will not attempt to alter them.

- Because you should not clean the coins yourself, you must take them to a professional coin cleaning service. They use a technique known as "dipping" to clean the coins without reducing their value. This is especially important if the coin's date and details cannot be determined due to corrosion.

- If you must clean the coin you have discovered, use the least harmful method possible. Don't use harsh chemicals, sulfuric acid, polishing cloth, vinegar, abrasive pastes, or devices that give the coin a smooth and shiny finish. Experiment with lower-value coins first, then move on to higher-value coins.

Cleaning is a major issue in coin collecting, so if you are selling a coin you know has been cleaned, you must disclose this to the buyer.

Protecting Your Collection from Loss by Fire or Theft

There will always be the threat of loss by fire or theft to any of your properties. However, just as you would protect your house or car from them, there are several precautions you can take to minimize them. Bear in mind that most homeowner insurance excludes coins and other items of numismatic value from coverage. You can usually get a rider, however, but for an additional premium payment.

A separate policy can also be obtained. Consider joining the American Numismatic Association (ANA), which provides insurance for its members' coin collections. Make a catalog of your collection and keep it separate from the coins. Take note of where you got each coin, its condition, and the price you paid for it.

Taking close-up photos of each coin is also a good idea. Get an appraisal from a Blue Book or Red Book professional. The insurance company will require the appraisal documents.

Safes protect your belongings from theft, fire, dust, water, and other environmental factors. They provide some protection for your coins. Some safes offer adequate fire protection but are not suitable for theft protection. Safes that deter thieves exist, but they are not fireproof. Even if the flames do not come into contact with your coins, they can be damaged or destroyed. The heat could be intense enough to melt them.

Another issue to consider when storing your coins in a safe is humidity. A high level will result in oxidation, which is harmful to the coins. The ideal relative humidity level is 30%. (RH). The ambient RH determines the RH inside the safe in the area where the safe is located. Fortunately, most modern safes are adequately insulated and have good seals. Silica gel packets can aid in humidity reduction.

If you decide to keep your collection at home, make sure you get a safe home that provides adequate fire and humidity protection and protection against theft. Take precautions to deter or prevent a burglar from entering your home. It is recommended that adequate lighting and secure, strong locks be used. You can get more useful information from law enforcement officers.

Being discreet about being a coin collector is one way to protect your investment from theft. The information you share about yourself with many people may eventually reach the wrong person. Having all numismatic promotional materials sent to a post office box rather than your home address may help.

Coin collections have a long and rich history; you must store your coins properly to preserve that heritage. When it comes time to sell your coins, properly preserved coins will be worth more and offer more money to your heirs. Mints produce coins from metal; except for gold, most will respond unfavorably to several environmental variables. Copper and silver are two of the most popular metals used in coinage. These are also some of the metals with the highest chemical reactivity. You may devise a defensive strategy to defend your collection if you know your adversary.

Causes of Damage

Although most metal is a durable substances, several variables can affect the state of your coins. Many coin collectors store their coins for extended periods without ever inspecting them. Checking on the state of your coins in storage regularly is one of the greatest strategies to prevent harm from occurring.

Humidity

The most dangerous enemy of a coin is humidity. Copper and silver coins are among the most frequent metals used in coin manufacture. Unfortunately, when these two metals come into touch with water, they will react chemically. Water vapor is present in varying degrees all around us and can infiltrate almost everything. Unfortunately, this is one of the most difficult environmental sources of coin damage to prevent. Some businesses promote coin holders as "airtight," although this is not a guarantee.

Heat and Cold

Heat, by itself, does not always cause coin damage. However, it shortens the time it takes for a coin to be harmed by other environmental conditions, including humidity, acids, and air pollution. On the other hand, cold can harm the delicate surface of uncirculated coins when moisture condenses into liquid water and deposits itself on the coin's surface.

Acids

Acids are derived from a variety of sources. The most prevalent source of acid is coin collection materials made of paper and cardboard that were acid-treated during production. These acids will leach out of the paper or cardboard over time, causing toning and tarnish, particularly on copper and silver coins. Acids can be emitted by adhesives used in packaging. Another source of acid is wood furniture and common home products such as cleaning solutions and cooking gasses. Avoid putting your coin collection in a cupboard that houses cleaning products or other chemicals.

Chlorine

Chlorine triggers a chemical reaction that degrades the look of your coins. This might range from mild ugly toning to corrosion-causing pits on the coin's surface. One of the primary causes of this is flips manufactured of PVC-containing plastic (polyvinyl chloride). Furthermore, gases from a hot tub or pool might infiltrate the space where your coin collection is kept.

Air Pollution

Air pollution is not only damaging to our health, but it is also harmful to the health of our coin collections. Air pollution is primarily a concern in densely populated regions, as haze from automobiles may concentrate and enter the surrounding buildings. Steps have been taken over the years to limit the number of toxic gases emitted by cars, but they might still exist in sufficient quantities to destroy a coin. Avoid putting your coins near a garage or a storage place containing petroleum materials.

Improper Handling

The most avoidable sort of coin damage is caused by improper handling. Directly touching a coin with your fingers can leave deposits of acids and oils on the surface, causing it to deteriorate.

Taking Care of Collectible Coins

Avoid storing your coins on a high, shaky shelf where they might fall over. Use a two-pocket box made of Polyester, designed specifically for storing coins, if you intend to display them on show.

Cleaning of Coins

Over time, coins can accumulate a lot of grime. Numerous strategies provide excellent cleaning solutions, whether you are trying to lighten up your old coins or put a sheen to make them valuable. Still, even before you continue, you should ask yourselves if you should wash your coins.

Wear a Mask

While wearing a mask is not strictly necessary, you should be conscious of your actions. When you breathe or talk, moisture from your mouth can get onto your coins without realizing it.

Keeping your coins in an airtight container with purified water and sand is a simple way to clean your regular pocket change. To brighten your money, simply seal the container and shake it firmly. This approach, however, depends on abrasion and is not recommended for precious, ancient, or collector coins.

Seek the Advice of a Professional

Always consult with a reputable coin grading service before cleaning your collectible coins. Cleaning collectible coins can significantly reduce their value; however, coin "toning," or the coloration and tarnishing caused by air exposure, can also contribute to their overall value. As a result, cleaning valuable or antique coins is not always advised.

It is best to grip ancient coins on the edges rather than the face when holding them. Oils and fingerprints can reduce a coin's value. Because coin grading is regulated, even the smallest blemish from swiping a one-off can significantly reduce its value.

Using a cotton swab, apply a layer of Vaseline or any other lubricant. Gently dab the coin with a specialized lint-free cloth to remove the lubricant. This is a method of removing unwanted dirt or dust without affecting the coin's value. When doing this, use a magnifying glass with caution. Apply the Vaseline with a q-tip and a very delicate non-synthetic brush. Avoid smearing too much Vaseline on the coin. The key is to apply the thinnest layer possible.

Immerse coins in acetone for 5 seconds. Using any methanol on your coin can give it a brownish tint and significantly reduce its value. You must immediately rinse your coins with distilled water to remove all traces of acetone before allowing them to air dry. Only use a soft cloth to clean or rub your ancient coins. Because acetone is a solution, not an acid, it will not devalue your coins until they are exposed to it for an extended period.

Acetone is a flammable liquid. If you decide to use this chemical, wear powder-free gloves. If you're using a distilled water jar, line the bottom with a napkin, so your coins don't get scratched when they come into contact with each other inside the jar. Use only 100 percent pure acetone. Other acetone-containing items will contain additional compounds that devalue your currency.

Keeping Your Coins Safe

How would you keep your coins safe and secure now that you have them? We have spoken about handling coins safely not to get damaged. Now we must decide whether or not to maintain these coins in our possession and whether or not to do so again to protect them from danger.

Whether you have found some fine circulation coins or bought some from a reputable dealer, you will need a way to keep them safe from damage. There are a variety of ways that damage might occur. It is much more than getting two or more coins that rub against one another in your Numismatics, which would be a no-no in and of itself. Scratches, nicks, and gouges are common effects of this type of damage, but your valuable coins can also be harmed in other ways.

Corrosion, fingerprint spots from atmospheric moisture droplets, and dark toning are only a few types of deterioration in coin collecting. Natural fading on a silver coin, such as a bloom of champagne or gold color, can be magnificent. The damage we are talking about is commonly a result of a coin being exposed to specific air conditions or stored incorrectly. Maybe the proprietor tried cleaning it with a solvent not meant for coins. In any case, a coin can acquire an unattractive black or other dark color. Soaking such a coin frequently leads to additional deterioration.

FAQ and Common Mistakes with Coins

Why Should I Keep Track of My Coins?

You have a coin catalog that includes the date of purchase, the purchase amount, and who sold the coin to you, right?

Many coin collectors I know feel driven to keep track of their holdings. Others toss the pennies into a bag, box, or old Mason jar and set them aside. Keeping track of your coins is a crucial element of the pastime. The IRS requires you to keep your coin purchases and sales for taxation. The IRS may presume anything on the spot when there are no records. The coin's worth is profit, so it's taxable. If you have amassed a sizable collection yet haven't kept even the most essential records, it won't be a pretty picture when the IRS finds out. Another reason to keep track of your coins is to assist your heirs. If something were to happen to you, your estate would be an excellent place to start. Keeping a coin catalog will make sure they won't throw out your collection while thinking it isn't anything important.

What if I Don't Have Any Records of my Coins?

You don't have to keep a catalog if you don't want to. But keeping a well-kept record helps you keep your coins on track. It'll also help your future heirs, so they don't get sidetracked when it's time to get rid of them.

Ways to Catalog Coins

There are several different methods used by coin collectors I know to keep track of their coin collection. Some record all the information on standard 3x5 cards stuck in a shoebox. Others use coin collecting software with sophisticated databases.

There is no one best way to catalog your coin collection. They are, after all, your coins, and you should use a method that you find comfortable. It should also be a method that you will use consistently and regularly.

What you keep track of is essential too. Here's the shortlist I use for all of my collections:

- Country of Origin
- Year of Mint
- Denomination
- Grade
- Date of Purchase
- Purchase Price
- Date Sold
- Sale Price

If you regularly buy and sell rolls, you may want to have a column for "Quantity." Another possibility is if you're buying variety or error coins, you'll want to have a column to include that information.

You could use a notebook with a pen and a straight edge to create the necessary columns. Since most of us own a computer, you likely own spreadsheet software like Microsoft Excel or possibly OpenOffice.

Either of these programs makes it simple to create a comprehensive means of tracking your coin collection, including calculating the value of individual coins.

Coin Collecting Software

I've chosen coin collecting software with an integrated database to track my coins and keep their values up to date. There are several different software packages available. Some are free, most reasonably priced, and others a bit more expensive. As in all things, you get what you pay for. You could even build your database using Microsoft Access which is included in premium versions of Microsoft Office.

Coin collecting software should be:

- Easy to use
- Intuitive
- Easy to organize your collections
- Ability to retrieve current pricing
- Automatically updates your coin values

Coin collecting software can save time and ease the burden of cataloging your coin collection. Is it necessary for everyone? You're the only one who can answer that.

Keeping track of your coins in a simple spreadsheet may be your best solution. One of the things you now know? You *do* need to be cataloging your coin collection.

How can You Monetize Your Coin Collection Hobby?

Whether you started your coin collection as a hobby or as an investment, there will come a time when you consider selling the coins you have accumulated. You might need to because of a personal financial need or perhaps help a relative or a friend. You will surely not sell them because you have tired of them and lost interest.

Just like any commodity, you expect a fair price to be offered for them, and you also expect to profit somehow from the sale, no matter how small it will be. You have several options when it comes to selling your collection.

You can choose to go by the route of a public auction. Most auction houses, however, have a minimum consignment value. And if yours is below this figure, they will not accept your collection. You will need to find another dealer accepting lesser-value coins and auctioning them for you quickly. Another way to sell your collection is through a personal sale.

Conclusion

Thank you for reading this book. People collect coins for a variety of reasons. Some people collect because they are drawn to the historical aspect of their hobby. Every coin collected represents a unique piece of the daily lives of people who lived decades, if not centuries ago. While some people collect coins for investment or profit, the collection of coins grows in value over time.

Whatever your reason or motive, whether one of the above or another personal and peculiar one, I hope this book has helped you find a way to start and some hints to move your first steps into this beautiful journey confidently.

Coin collecting takes up a lot of time. As a result, be patient and pay attention to quality. Coin collectors can learn much about history, metal, and other subjects. It's an exciting time to be a numismatist right now.

Coin collecting is an investment as well. Investing in coins is a simple way to diversify a person's financial portfolio. It is a straightforward method of protecting against inflation and economic uncertainty.

Coin clubs can help you broaden your knowledge base while providing you with the most up-to-date information on collectible coins. Don't forget that your best asset is your equipment and other coin collectors.

A big part of becoming a successful coin collector is learning about it and constantly discovering new information as it emerges. Sign up for a local coin club if one exists in your area. Look for coin collecting groups on the internet. This could be a great networking opportunity for you and a chance to meet someone with a coin you want. The more people you know who enjoy coin collecting, the more opportunities you'll have to add to your collection while also making some money. Remember that knowledge and experience are essential for coin collecting success.

Coin collecting is more than just collecting coins; it is also about discovering and learning about history through coins and other collectibles without ever leaving your house.

Many people are drawn to collecting as a treasure hunt because loose change can conceal some surprises. There are still coins in circulation that are old enough to be worth more than face value, and in some cases, much more.

On the internet, look for coin collecting clubs. This can be a great networking opportunity and a chance to meet someone with the coin you're looking for. The more coin collectors you know, the more opportunities you'll have to expand your collection while potentially earning money.

Coin collecting is viable for various reasons and isn't all that difficult. The best part is that it can help you in various ways. If you enjoy history, art, and beauty, you can do it as a part-time hobby. On the other hand, if you thoroughly review the fundamentals, you can turn it into a profitable activity.

Whatever your reason or motive, whether one of the aforementioned or something more personal and one-of-a-kind. This book has helped you find a way to start and guide you in taking your first bold steps into this beautiful adventure. This book will teach you about coin types and anatomy. Of course, this is just the start of your new interest.

Happy collecting!

Made in the USA
Thornton, CO
07/29/24 19:09:34

43468548-cf3d-4951-8065-40fc3c7ea7a3R01